Family Energetics

DEBORAH H. DONNDELINGER

Copyright © 2012 by Deborah H. Donndelinger
All Rights Reserved
ISBN-13: 978-1480246553
ISBN-10: 1480246557

First Edition: December 2012
Published in the United States

Cover design by Logoglo.com
Drawings by Suzanne Brault of Eldersburg, Maryland
Formatting, editing, and layout by PixelHappyStudio.com
Proofreading by Karen McLaughlin of Hamilton, Ontario
Handwriting font © 2006 by Vimala Rodgers and IIHS.com

Dedication

To the children we once were, the children who are now, and the children yet to come.

Foreword

My heartfelt soul's desire is to contribute to a world where all children feel safe. The cornerstone of this vision is that every adult feels vibrant, empowered, connected, and loving. Once the adults have their act together, we can dramatically change how children are seen and treated.

There are many paths to what I call "getting our act together". For some of us, working with what is called the family matrix is an integral part of this path to ease and connection.

If you find yourself curious or attracted to this work, I expect that you will find Family Energetics to be an awesome tool that helps you. And if you find that the material feels restrictive or annoys you, trust your instincts and wait for another time or perhaps pass the book on to someone else.

I have four personal criteria for this book:

- Have I explained the concepts in a way that is understandable?
- Does the work do justice to the spiritual concept of oneness?
- Does this work offer tools that expand your thinking?
- Does this work offer ideas that empower others in their spiritual and healing journey?

You might not agree with everything that's been written, but if the work sparks one new idea or insight that shows you the love that is available in both your family system and in you, then I will consider the many hours of labor to have indeed been worthwhile.

With much love,

Deborah Donndelinger

Table of Contents

Chapter One: Introducing Family Energetics..........................1
    What Are We Looking For?..1
    The Missing Piece Is at the Family Level............................2
    The Ancestral Flow of Life...3
    My Story..4
    The Conception of Family Energetics..................................6
    What Is Family Energetics? 8
    Respects...9
    Boundaries...9
    What Is Not in This Book..10
Chapter Two: The Basics...11
    The Use of EFT in This Work...11
    The EFT Procedure..12
        Set-Up..12
        The Rounds...13
    Three Options for Tapping..15
    Setting Up the Exercise...16
    Family Matrix..17
    When to Use Family Energetics.......................................17
    In a Nutshell 18
    What to Expect...19
        Today's Date...20
Chapter Three: Foundational Principles................................23

Systems Optimize to Be Whole and Healthy 24
We as Individuals Are Components of a Family System ...25
System Health over Individual Health 26
The Path to Healing Is Seeing the Excluded Parts..............26
Our Individual Symptoms Are Not Personal......................27
This Work Can Heal the Past...27
EFT Can Ease the Way...28

Chapter Four: Guidance for Exercises......................................29
Sense, Imagine, and Experience: The Use of Intuition......29
Responsibility..29
Relief to Tension..30
What Shows Up Is Helpful and of Service 30
Family Matrix Information Is Available to Us 31
System Information, Not Yours 32
Appropriate Phrases...32
Closing the Exercises..33

Chapter Five: General Exercises..35
Your Parents..35
Your Mother..44
Your Father..49
    The Previous Generation...53
    Your Father's Line...53
    Your Mother's Line...55
Grandparents..57
Disconnection in Family Lineage..61

Chapter Six: Working with Specifics.................................65
   Where to Start..66
Chapter Seven: Homelands and Loss............................69
   When We Leave Our Homelands....................................69
   When We Are Forced to Leave: Enslavement................74
   War...79
   Early or Unexpected Losses..87
   Family Lore, Unusual Events, Crimes, and Black Sheep.....94
Chapter Eight: Love and Loss..99
   First Loves...100
   Later Partners...105
   Divorce..110
   Children from New Relationships..................................114
Chapter Nine: Children and Loss.................................121
   Children's Order...122
   Missing Twin...127
   Miscarriage...132
   Adoption..136
      Biological Parents and the Child................................136
      Adoptive Parents and the Biological Parents...............140
   Terminated Pregnancies..145
      The Mother's Perspective..146
      From the Mother to the Father..................................150
      Mother to Child..153
   No Children...156

Chapter Ten: Fate, Connection, and Appreciation..............161
   Feeling Stuck and Not Understanding............................161
   Uncomfortable Secrets..166
   Great-Grandparents Connection....................................171

Afterword..182
   What Is Possible...182
   With Appreciation 183
      My Family..183
      My Colleagues and Friends.....................................184
      My Teachers..184
   About the Author..186

Chapter One: Introducing Family Energetics

What Are We Looking For?

Many people today are looking to feel more complete and at ease in their lives. They use different healing, self-development, and spiritual methods trying to feel "better" physically, emotionally, mentally, and spiritually. Some of it works; some of it does not. I know that for myself over the past twenty-some years, I have studied and applied a variety of modalities trying to feel more at ease with myself and trying to develop myself into some unknown yet ultimate potential.

An obvious, and to me ironic, trap exists in this desire to grow. Ultimately we do not have to fix anything. At the core of the quest to feel better is what folks call "spiritual enlightenment" or what I call spiritual truth. Byron Katie beautifully describes this experience in her book where she writes:

> "All my rage, all the thoughts that had been troubling me, my whole world, the whole world, was gone. At the same time, laughter welled up from the depths and just poured out. Everything was unrecognizable. It was as if something else had woken up. It opened its eyes. It was looking through Katie's eyes. And it was so delighted! It was intoxicated with joy. There was nothing separate, nothing unacceptable to it; everything was its very own self."[1]

---

[1] Byron Katie, *Loving What Is*, (New York, New York: Three Rivers Press, 2002), p. x-xi.

The veil that separates us from the Divine drops and we experience momentarily, or perhaps forever, Universal Love. And that is the true purpose of any healing or spiritual modality: to help us reconnect with our sense of Universal Love and to know that love is always available to and through us, and in fact is who we are.

Yet only a few of us have had enlightening experiences that change our lives forever. The rest of us keep doing the work, step-by-step, piece-by-piece, clearing the blocks to our ease.

And indeed we do the work. We clear trauma, we look at patterns in our behavior, and we learn to love ourselves. But we still do not feel happy, successful, or complete.

The Missing Piece Is at the Family Level

The missing piece is often found at the next level of organization, the family system, or what I call the family matrix. On the personal level, we have learned to see our reactive egoic defense mechanisms that built up as a result of past experiences. These structures are designed to protect us from something outside of ourselves but ultimately limit us and keep us reactive. We can see and address these blocks when we do our spiritual and personal healing.

Likewise, our family systems also have reactive defensive structures in place that are designed to protect the family. Like a healing scab can turn into an ugly mess of scar tissue, so can these defense structures constrict the flow of energy throughout the family matrix resulting in what feels like an ugly mess. The challenge is that we do not always know how to heal at this level when it involves places and events beyond our direct experience.

I will show you how to reconnect. At its essence, this book is an invitation to connect to the love that is available at the core of our families and our ancestral lineage. On a practical level, this book is a guide providing you tools to heal specific blocking events in your family's past.

Just as every single one of us is a unique expression of Universal Love, every single one of our families and ancestors is also a unique expression of this creative force. This book is about how to reclaim and reconnect to that love of our ancestors and place. Our hearts want to belong. But how do we belong to a family that has secrets or pain or abuse or loss? Let us find out together.

You have the ability to reconnect with the strong ancestral heritage that is both your birthright and your heart's desire. Whether you come from a family with obvious flaws and challenges such as addiction, abuse, or early-deaths or whether you come from a family with unnamed and unseen secrets, you have the opportunity now to unravel the energetic blocks that limit your success, your happiness, and your sense of ease today.

The Ancestral Flow of Life

Imagine love flowing from one generation to the next, from older to younger, generation to generation. Imagine that love rooted in one's homeland, reaching forward through the generations, feeding, nourishing, and expanding. Imagine the love flowing from parent to child, parent to child.

And then it stops. No next child comes. No connection exists between parent and child. Only walls and dams and barren stretches exist, caused by loss and war, failed relationships, and lost children. The connection has been broken and we think it

Chapter One

is our fault. The connection has been broken and we think it is our family's fault.

This book is a guide to the process of releasing and healing any constriction that comes from who we think we are and how we experience our family of origin and our ancestral roots. This process is a loving and healing practice taken one step at a time until the cascade of love rushes in and all the walls and boundaries fall away and we see the perfection of both who we are and where we came from.

My Story

Since Family Energetics is about seeing the past and its path, allow me to share mine. I am 45 years old as I write this book. My journey to this book has followed a windy yet purposeful path.

I was born in the United States in the late sixties, moved to Europe when I was three years old, and lived there for eight years. I am the firstborn with one younger brother and two younger half-sisters. My parents divorced when I was young and my father remarried.

I was moved around a lot in both the States and Europe and I spent a handful of years part-time in Saudi Arabia. One grandparent was born and raised in Germany and the others were born in the States and are of Northern European lineage.

After earning both Bachelors and Masters of Science in Industrial Engineering and Operations Research, I worked as a reliability engineer at an aerospace consulting company. During my time there, I was tasked to become an internal quality management resource and became skilled at teaching and facilitating teams as they analyzed and improved their work processes.

Along the way a dearly loved mentor of mine introduced me to the Enneagram, a spiritual model that to this day still informs my personal and professional work. The Enneagram was my initiation into the world of spiritual development. I continued my quality facilitation and training career and took a position at a medical system. I became more and more interested in how my personal strengths and development impacted my professional work and eventually studied at National Training Lab and earned a certification in Organization Development.

After meeting and marrying my husband, I became pregnant with my son and when he was born stopped my professional life to be at home. His birth ignited in me a passion for trusting my intuition.[2] Some health challenges along the way with my firstborn introduced me to homeopathy and other forms of energy medicine. We were on the Feingold diet and allergies played a significant role in his health issues.[3]

I started working with energy based modalities as a way to help my son. I also found myself sharing what I was learning with other mothers and put together my first website called Energetic Mothers. As I started working with other mothers and clients using Emotional Freedom Techniques (EFT), I become aware of how powerful EFT is in healing emotional traumas and also that I had a skill in seeing what the underlying issues are. But sometimes I was thwarted. I just

---

[2] Readers might recall the article "A Wake Up Call" where I write about this. http://www.eftwithdeborah.com/a-wake-up-call

[3] The Feingold program is an approach where artificial preservatives, colors and foods high in salicylates are removed from the diet with sometimes significant improvements in speech, behavior and other allergy-based symptoms. http://www.feingold.org/

Chapter One

could not make inroads on some personal and client issues despite persistent and thorough tapping.

The Conception of Family Energetics

As part of my studies, I attended an Allergy Antidotes workshop, a multi-day training on different energy modalities that can be used to clear allergy-like sensitivities.[4] At the training we talked about emotional components of allergies and how hidden emotional aspects can sometimes block treatment of sensitivities.

A fellow participant, Kim, mentioned how hidden family loyalties can contribute to allergies and other health issues. I had already done a lot of work around allergies with mixed results so was intrigued by her comment. I also have a strong family history of allergies and started wondering about other ways of clearing my family legacy.

The field of work Kim was referring to is commonly called Family Constellations. I found a Family Constellations trainer and dove deeply into learning more. After attending various workshops and trainings for a year or two, I then decided to commit to an extended course of study and earned my facilitator certification in an intense year-long process.[5] This work spoke to me immediately. Each and every workshop I attended, I experienced and witnessed radical shifts in life force energy as a direct result of working with a family constellation. As someone who is intuitive and sensitive to

---

[4] Sandi Radomski, founder of Allergy Antidotes, was one of the first EFT practitioners who realized we can use EFT to clear the effects of toxins and allergens. She has a wide body of work that I admire and respect. http://www.allergyantidotes.com/

[5] Hellinger Institute of DC, Bethesda, MD. http://www.hellingerdc.com/

emotions and energies, I experienced intense emotions and insights in many different representations of family systems. As someone with an analytical mind, I quickly saw the patterns and models underlying the work. The combination of these two attributes turned out to be vital in developing Family Energetics.

Family Constellations offers clear insights into stubborn problems. It is traditionally done in groups, and representatives are an integral element of the work. At that time I was working exclusively by phone, growing my EFT business, and wanted to keep using EFT with all its unique advantages.

I found some of the concepts from Family Constellations influencing my tapping work and began to experiment with combining both modalities in my work with clients. What quickly became clear is that both fields together are synergistically powerful, so I started intentionally and deliberately combining the two, calling the work Family Energetics.

The results and feedback from clients and colleagues were encouraging. Folks from the meridian tapping world gravitated towards the principles from Family Constellations and found relief to stubborn problems that EFT had not been able to address. Results included improved relationships with family members long estranged, peace from long ago abortions, acceptance of failed marriages, life brought back to current marriages, success to failing businesses, and personal peace after long-standing unease.

My clients were not newcomers to the healing world; they were other EFT practitioners, psychotherapists, and therapists, all smart, educated, motivated people. This book came about because clients and practitioners keep asking for more

Chapter One

information about Family Energetics. Both bodies of work are tremendous, but combined, a synergy exists that wants to be seen and heard.

What Is Family Energetics?

Family Energetics is the unique blending of Family Constellations and Emotional Freedom Techniques into a loving and effective approach for unraveling family entanglements that block our path today. These blocks can show up differently in each person's life and include physical, interpersonal, family, and work issues. Family Constellations brings the theory, models, and language to help us see our family history in a new way; EFT brings a hands-on tool that makes the process more manageable, less painful, and more effective in individual applications.

For EFT practitioners, an opportunity exists to expand our methods and to increase our clients' results. Interest is growing in the EFT community in using meridian techniques to address ancestral patterns; however, **if the hidden dynamics of these ancestral patterns are not viewed with the proper perspective, understanding, respect, and ultimately love, the desired results and freedom will not be achieved.** Just as the EFT set-up phrase has us accept and love ourselves even though we have our issues, the goal of looking at our family matrix is to ultimately love and accept our ancestors and family even though we have these family patterns.

Similarly, the world of Family Constellations can benefit from the world of energy meridian work. The stress in constellations can be considerable and EFT eases that process while supporting the underlying re-connections wanting to be made.

Respects

Family Constellation is the common name for the work developed by Bert Hellinger who has a rich and varied past including his war-time experiences in Germany and his years in South Africa as a priest.[6] Family Constellations has deep roots and is both detailed and specific. EFT is a slightly newer method that is also based on previous work that reaches back through time with the work of Dr. Callahan, John Diamond, Dr. Goodheart and of course 5000 years of eastern medicine. I honor deeply the two lines of work that came together to create Family Energetics. Just like we are the products of co-creation along many generations, so is this work before you.

Boundaries

This work is for folks who are ready to take responsibility for their healing, trusting both the family matrix and their bodies for insights along the way. This work is an energy based approach to spiritual wholeness and connection.

This work is not therapy or a substitute for advice from a licensed health care practitioner. This work is not intended to replace Family Constellations workshops. This work is not the only application of EFT. This work is considered experimental and experiential in nature. I am an engineer by academic training and an energetic, spiritual healing guide by experience. I invite anyone interested to join me in this journey but with one condition. Trust yourself and your intuition.

---

[6] http://en.wikipedia.org/wiki/Bert_Hellinger (September, 2012).

Chapter One

What Is Not in This Book

Some topics are strikingly powerful, wide-ranging, systemic, and life-altering. These include: the Armenian genocide of World War I, the holocaust of World War II, any country's systemic wars, apartheid in South Africa, United States slavery, the massive atrocities against Native Americans, Aborigines, and other native people plus many more. I wish I could write for each of these areas but I do not have the privilege yet to do so. I acknowledge deeply the losses here and the ripples that are still asking to be seen and addressed.

I also have not included incest, suicide, mental illness, rape and sexual abuse. These themes are dear to my heart and I believe should be handled with love and care in a caring relationship with a professional. For help finding someone to work with on these areas, please contact me at: www.FamilyEnergetics.com.

Chapter Two: The Basics

This book is divided into several sections:

- General principles and introductory material (Chapters Two, Three, and Four).
- General yet comprehensive exercises that anyone can use regardless of their situation (Chapter Five).
- Guidance and tapping scripts for specific family situations (Chapters Six through Ten).

I suggest you read the general section first. Absorb what you can and then return a few times as you work on the other exercises. I find myself having new insights every time I read the Foundational Principles.

If you know of some specific events in your family, find the specific section that pertains to you. If you want to start at an overall level, the general exercises will get you started.

The Use of EFT in This Work

Pretty much every exercise here uses tapping, originally known as Emotional Freedom Techniques (EFT). EFT is the body of work founded by Gary Craig based on the body's energy system.[7] The premise of his work is that negative emotion is caused by disrupted energy in the body. He developed a robust, easy-to-use protocol that involves tapping on different

---

[7] Gary Craig has asked that EFT practitioners be clear that he does not endorse others' work and that while I have studied his material and earned several certifications in EFT, he as the founder of EFT in no way makes any guarantee or has any responsibility for my work here.

meridian points in the body. The lineage of EFT includes Dr. Roger Callahan of Thought Field Therapy, John Diamond, M.D., and Dr. George Goodheart.[8]

Mr. Craig developed two protocols in his original work: a short cut protocol which is more commonly used today and the longer version which includes the gamut point.[9] I use the short-cut version in this book; however, if you are not noticing results from tapping using the short-cut recipe, please consider adding in the gamut point procedure.[10]

The EFT Procedure

The EFT procedure has two parts that use different wording: the set-up phrase and the rounds. The set-up phrases are said while tapping on the karate chop points and the rounds are done while tapping on eight specific points, rotating through one point at a time while saying short phrases.

Set-Up

The karate chop points shown in Illustration 1 are used for the set-up. While tapping the karate points on the skinny edge of one hand, we say a phrase that has the format of:

Even though I have this issue, I deeply and completely love and accept myself.

---

[8] http://masteringeft.com/masteringblog/about-eft/history-of-eft/ (September, 2012)

[9] Craig, Gary. (2008). The EFT Manual. Santa Rosa, CA: Energy Psychology Press.

[10] http://www.eftwithdeborah.com/eft/eft-tapping-points has a video of the points and the gamut procedure.

Repeat three times while tapping on the karate chop points with the fingertips of the other hand.

Illustration 1: The Set-Up Points Also Known As the Karate Chop Points

The Rounds

After the set-up tapping is done, different parts of the face and torso are tapped on while saying a phrase. Each point is tapped on by itself so you are tapping sequentially on eight different points on the body. Tap each point with your fingertips, tapping five to seven times per point. All points are on bone. Tap with some emphasis but not so hard that you hurt yourself.

The head points, shown in Illustration 2, are the eyebrow, the side of the eye, under the eye, under the nose, chin, collarbone, and under the arm. A point is often included on the crown of the head.[11]

---

[11] The head point was not originally included in the EFT protocol. After Michael Grady of the East-West Healing Arts Center in Oakland California taught at one of Gary Craig's advanced topic workshops, people started including the head point as it touches on several meridian paths. This demonstration can be found in the DVD called Steps to Becoming the Ultimate Therapist by Gary Craig released in 1998.

Chapter Two

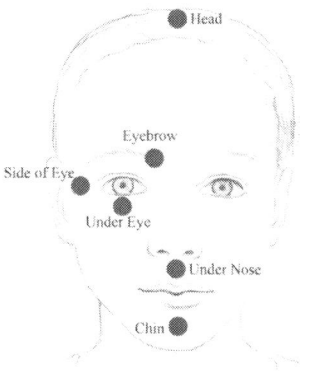

Illustration 2: Six Points Are on the Head

Specifically, the **eyebrow** point is located at the beginning of either eyebrow near the bridge of the nose on the orbital bone. The point on the **side of the eye** is found by following the eyebrow around to its end, near the outside of either eye, on the bone, in front of the temple. The **under the eye** point is on the orbital bone still, directly underneath the pupil. The **nose** point is under the nose, on the "mustache" area. The **chin** point is between the lower lip and the chin, in the crease below the lip. The **head** point is on the crown of the head.

The Basics

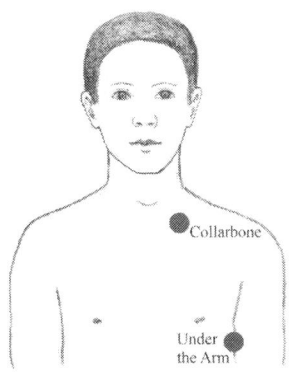

Illustration 3: The Two Torso Points

The torso points, shown in Illustration 3, are on the collarbone and under the arm. The **collarbone** is actually just below the collarbone, one inch down and to the right or left of the notch in the throat. The **under the arm** point is four inches below the armpit, along the side of the body.

Three Options for Tapping

In this book, I provide three different formats for your tapping. You can do only one or you can do all three. The three are:

1. A **Reiterative Tapping** script where specific phrases are repeated. I provide the suggested words. This is the simplest and can be the most thorough for the specific issue.

2. A **Cascading Tapping** script where the language flows and varies as we move through the points. I provide the language. If the language fits your situation, this option can cover more aspects of the situation. This might mean there is more

Chapter Two

clearing but also might mean you need to do some more tapping by yourself on the specific aspects.

3. An **Intuited Tapping** where you follow your own language inspired by what you have read. This is appropriate when you feel that your own words will provide the insight into the tension in the system.

Setting Up the Exercise

If you have experience with family constellations done in groups or with figures, the format of the exercises will feel familiar to you. If you have not seen a constellation done in a group or with figures, let me explain a bit more. In a group constellation, different people stand in for the family members in the constellation.

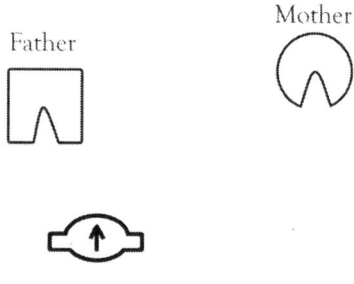

Illustration 4: Self with Parents

For example, if you are working with the energy between you, your mother, and your father, three people would be chosen and positioned in the room according to what the energy feels like. A configuration might look like what is shown in Illustration 4.

The illustration shows you that you are facing the general direction of your parents but feel closer to your father. Your father is looking past you and your mother is looking at someone or something else.

When doing this sort of work by ourselves and adding in tapping, we will not be using other representatives for our family members. Instead we will use our senses, our intuition, and our imagination to virtually set-up these configurations. I will provide example diagrams so that you can imagine where the different people would be placed in the virtual set-up.

Family Matrix

The term "matrix" has varying meanings in the energy psychology world. I use the term "family matrix" to mean the family system which includes living and dead family members of many generations, persons tied to each family through significant events and actions, and the complete set of ancestral homelands. This matrix has no clear beginning or end, and, like a crystal diffusing light into a rainbow, each person's matrix is centered and shaped from his unique configuration.

When to Use Family Energetics

- You have done EFT or other energy work on issues and are not getting the results you want.
- You notice patterns or themes over time in your relationships or in work that you want to shift.
- You find yourself overreacting to family members or significant others and you know it is out of proportion to the issue.

- You have a sense that a family system component is hindering your sense of place and ease in the world.

In a Nutshell

When we do personal healing work, we often are doing one of the following:

- Identifying and clearing trauma from our childhood or adult lives.
- Looking at personal behavioral, cognitive, or emotional patterns that block our success.
- Looking at hidden defense mechanisms that make us reactive.
- Seeing and integrating our shadow traits.
- Loving and accepting ourselves.

Working with the family matrix is doing the exact same thing, except we are moving up one organizational level from the individual to the family. So we are:

- Identifying and clearing traumas from our family system.
- Looking at behavioral, cognitive, emotional, and energetic patterns that block our success.
- Seeing and integrating our family's shadow traits and triggers.
- Learning to accept and love where we come from and who we are.

What to Expect

Immediately after a Family Energetics exercise, you might feel relaxed, relieved, lighter, and perhaps tired. A sense of completion, inclusion, satisfaction, and connection is both immediate and long-lasting.

Other more tangible results come over time, sometimes several years later. I know, several years sounds like a long time personally but is not in the grand scheme of things. I have been fortunate to be in touch with clients seven years after their work and I have seen them make beautiful shifts in their lives. I cannot claim that Family Energetics was the only contributing factor; that would be arrogant. I have no doubt, however, that working with the family matrix in a kind and loving way has been part of the solution.

What I have noticed in clients is:

- A sense of ease in family relationships that was not apparent before.
- A distancing in relationships that were toxic or damaging.
- A change in job status for the better.
- A change in marital status for the better.
- More outward action aligned with a sense of self and one's purpose in the world.
- Resolution to health issues.

In fact, the changes can be so complete that some people forget what their lives were like before they started doing this Family Energetics work. If you want to track your progress over the years, I invite you to make a few notes about the general state of your life.

Today's Date

The top three concerns I have overall about my life:

1.

2.

3.

I am most appreciative about these three areas:

1.

2.

3.

How at ease do I feel in my body?

How "clean" are my family relationships? Where do I feel entangled or reactive?

How satisfied am I with my creative expression in life either through my work, my passions, or my children?

How much do I feel my sense of place in the world?

Thank you for doing this assessment. I find it invaluable to reflect over time on my journey and I trust you will as well. And now, on to some foundational material.

Chapter Three: Foundational Principles

No problem can ever be solved at the consciousness that created it. We must learn to see the world anew.

Albert Einstein

I invite you to contemplate deeply the following points. I believe that you will quickly notice the far-reaching implications.

- We as individuals are members of a system that includes several generations past as well as people strongly impacted by those generations.

- Systems optimize to be whole *and* healthy. When forced to choose, the system will choose completeness over health of its parts.

- The path to healing is seeing and including, from a place of love and flow, the excluded parts.

- We have mistakenly believed that our individual symptoms are personal.

- Our work today can shift the past.

- EFT can dramatically ease the way for us as we integrate with our family matrix.

Chapter Three

Systems Optimize to Be Whole and Healthy

When I taught organizational quality management back in the 90's, I developed a hands-on exercise to demonstrate systems thinking. [12] A mobile made of rods and strings in a multi-level pattern, similar to a baby's mobile, was the structure. Each person in the exercise was given a task that involved moving, adding, or deleting pegs from the mobile. Some folks had tasks that directly contradicted others' tasks. Nobody knew explicitly what the others' tasks were. No talking was allowed between participants to represent interdepartmental communication gaps.

Participants had five minutes to "do their task". A flurry of activity showed people putting pegs on, taking pegs off, and moving pegs to other levels. What quickly became apparent is that folks wanted both to accomplish their task AND also inherently wanted to keep the mobile balanced. They noticed the movement of the pegs overall and would sacrifice their own task in order to restore balance to the mobile itself. This bears repeating: **they sub-optimized their own task in order to keep the balance of the whole.**

My colleagues and I were pleased by this result. We were not sure if folks would focus solely on their task or, as we had hoped, intrinsically strive for maintaining the overall balance of this exercise. With such a visual of the mobile, the balance was quite obvious. Participants could see the entire system, and while they did not know each other's individual task, they

---

[12] Published in The 1999 Team & Organization Development Sourcebook, Editor Mel Silberman.

were willing to make compromises to keep the system balanced.

A Result with Hopeful Implications

In traditional departments, most people go for the optimization of their task at the expense of the system because they cannot see the larger system goal or purpose or the impact of their actions. In this experiential exercise, they optimized the system because they could see the overall impact of their actions and others' actions.

Likewise, in our family systems, we have similar roles, compromises and a desire for system health. But we are initially limited because we cannot see the entire system even though it is still impacting us.

Insights from this exercise directly apply to our Family Energetics work today.

- A system has an inherent intelligence to optimize its health.
- Individuals can be sacrificed for the sake of the whole.
- Most components do not see the system so do not understand the actions of others or even themselves.

We as Individuals Are Components of a Family System

Once we start looking beyond ourselves to the family matrix, we open up to a whole new field of healing. Once we realize that we are connected to our ancestors in ways we are only just beginning to understand, we see all the ways to move forward. It is a fundamental paradigm shift that has much potential. We are members of a system that includes former partners, perpetrators and victims, lost children, homelands, and so on. When one element of the system is suffering, often another segment of the system needs attention.

System Health over Individual Health

Time and time again, in every constellation I have seen and in every Family Energetics session I have conducted, the cause of the energetic entanglement in the family system is an unseen part of the matrix causing dysfunction in the system. This unseen part might be a person not acknowledged, an emotion not processed, or a connection not realized. The symptoms that you or the client are experiencing are a direct result of part of the matrix being choked off, confused, and not recognized. The system has a desire for completeness and balance and will sacrifice the function of some of its parts in order to achieve the inclusion of all parts.

Each of the scripts in the detailed chapters addresses common situations where the hidden element can be brought to light.

The Path to Healing Is Seeing the Excluded Parts

When this excluded part is introduced, seen, included, and recognized, the family system can realign to a whole state. This does not mean that the work is comfortable or that we are trying to make everything okay. It does mean that we are seeing what happened with new eyes and remaking connections long severed.

Our Individual Symptoms Are Not Personal

Many folks think, and indeed in the United States we are taught, that we are responsible for our own happiness. We see our personal happiness and contentment as a direct result of our own emotional health. We see ourselves as a tree in the forest, sharing space and air and light with the other trees but still feeling responsible for our own health.

Now imagine looking underground and seeing all the roots connected: sharing, nourishing, and supporting or strangling, choking and competing. Imagine seeing which root over there needs to be cut, which root over here needs to be reconnected, so that the entire forest can thrive.

When we see that the life situations and issues that have limited us are not personal but rather have a larger systemic cause, we experience a sense of hope and relief. Now a new avenue of exploration is opened and this path has the potential to bring us the ease we seek. When we expand our view to see the larger system, we can see the imbalance that we have wanted to heal. While our work is our own, the causes are not.

In fact, seeing our health as just personal can lead us away from our family of origin. When we disconnect from our family lineage, we are repeating the systemic reasons for unhappiness and the root cause is never seen and dealt with.

This Work Can Heal the Past

No matter how long someone has been dead, no matter what happened years ago, this work can change how the past affects us. By seeing what happened and making energetic shifts, we can bring relief to any situation. This might not make sense

Chapter Three

now, but trust me. Peace comes from seeing what is, what happened, who was included, who was cut out, and who needs to be included now. We do not erase the pain of war, or death, or loss, but instead illuminate it. **We can handle the pain. What we cannot handle is being disconnected.**

EFT Can Ease the Way

Those folks new to EFT do not know yet of the ease with which it can transform stuck energy, also known as emotions, into flow. One moment a person is consumed with grief, anger, or despair, and with a few taps, the emotion dissolves. If you do not use EFT already, be prepared for some surprises at what is possible. When using EFT in these exercises, we are not trying to fix what happened; we are clearing the disrupted energy in our systems as a result of what happened. Once we clear the disrupted energy, we are more open to seeing what is under those feelings.

Chapter Four: Guidance for Exercises

What follows is some guidance that will help you with the specific exercises that are in later chapters. You will also find it helpful for when you do your own intuited work.

Sense, Imagine, and Experience: The Use of Intuition

For each exercise here, you are invited to imagine, sense, experience, or intuit the family matrix or the field as it is called in constellations. I use the words sense, imagine, see, experience, or intuit interchangeably; however, each person has their own unique way of setting up the exercise. I personally do not actually see the participants; rather I have a non-specific kinesthetic sense of their presence.

The same is true when accessing the information for the system. You might get information from a body sensation or an emotional one. You might get it from a thought or an idea that appears. Be unabashed as you use what shows up in your experience.

What you notice might be very intense or it might be very subtle; neither one is better than the other. How you process information is unique to you; what matters is the distinction between tension and relief and we all know the difference.

Responsibility

You are doing this work on behalf of those who could not or did not. You have an interesting blend of responsibility. You are not responsible for feeling all the unprocessed emotions for

Chapter Four

the family matrix; however, by seeing the entanglements and acknowledging the events on behalf of your family, you are bringing relief to many.

Relief to Tension

One of the guiding sensations to notice is the sensation of tension and relief. When you are in the wrong place, saying the wrong healing words, or not seeing the complete picture, a feeling of tension constricts the body. Even though it might be painful or sad, seeing the complete picture and making the reconnection brings relief to the body. The signature sensation of relief guides you as you do this work. If you do not understand the words of a tapping script and they bring you relief, that is a sign you are on the right track. If you do not understand the words and they bring you tension, that is a sign there is more to uncover.

Paradoxically, if you look at a tapping script and feel tension or unease before beginning, that is a sign that the script might uncover something of value for you. In this case, tension is a sign that the work is asking to be done.

What Shows Up Is Helpful and of Service

People who have used EFT in different situations have learned to trust that intense emotions and memories can be neutralized pretty quickly with tapping. It is not trust per se but experience. As an EFT practitioner, I know that we can work through intense emotions and clear the response pretty quickly. I trust both the tool and my application of it. And I know that those intense feelings are a signpost to healing.

Similarly when working with the family matrix, emotions can be tapped into that are intense or that feel unsolvable. How can it possibly be helpful to look at an aborted child, a war victim, a murderer, the pain of a long distance separation, or ancestors who were enslaved? Just as we trust that all expressions of someone's internal world have something to offer us, and indeed show us a path to healing, we can trust that what is shown to us within the larger context of the family system can indeed be a path to healing.

Family Matrix Information Is Available to Us

This is one of the harder aspects of the field of Family Constellations to understand. If you have had the chance to attend a group workshop, you'll see representatives for different members of a family step into the field and experience emotions and thoughts that are not theirs. Somehow they tap into emotional and energetic information from the family of the person being worked.

Similarly, although often less intensely, in Family Energetics work we can tap into emotions, thoughts, and energies of family members further back in our ancestral line. This is not talking to the spirits or the dead. It is accessing information about their energy in their place in the family system. Some clients feel this energy quite clearly, some not quite so clearly. You do not have to feel the tension strongly to proceed. If you have any intuitive hit whatsoever that a tapping script appeals to you, and you approach it with respect and love, you can tap. All I ask is that you are open to the body responses you get, you do not attach to them, and that you stay loving and accepting of all that arises.

Chapter Four

System Information, Not Yours

If we open our minds to the idea that we can access information from other parts of the family matrix, we immediately shift the focus from "What is wrong?" to "How is this a symptom of the larger family system imbalance?" And while you might experience a variety of sensations in your body, I encourage you to view these sensations as system information and not personal. For example, if you tune into your grandfather's lineage and you experience sadness, that sadness is most likely tied to their destinies. Just because you feel it does not mean that it is your emotion.

Appropriate Phrases

Over time, the use of specific phrases has shown to be effective in Family Constellations. Some of these phrases feel antiquated but the gauge of their success is the relief that they bring. One of the trickiest phrases to avoid is "forgive". Other healing modalities often speak to forgiveness as a path to healing and wholeness. In the Family Constellation world, forgiveness brings in an element of "bigger than" energy and is a block to achieving system health.

John Payne has an excellent discussion on making apologies in his book *The Language of the Soul, Healing with Words of Truth*.[13] In fact, I recommend his book for all of its content.

I have included detailed phrasing for each tapping situation. If a phrase just does not feel right, try some of the other choices. Some generic phrases that might also be appropriate include:

---

[13] John L. Payne, *The Language of the Soul, Healing with Words of Truth*, (Findhorn, Scotland: Findhorn Press), p. 153.

- I see you now.
- I take responsibility for my part.
- Thank you for the gift of life.
- Bless me as I live my life.

As a general guideline in doing your own work, phrases that are energetically not helpful include:

- I am sorry.
- I forgive you.
- Any sentence starting with "You".

Closing the Exercises

Given that we are working with the energy of a system larger than us, it is appropriate to thank the field after working with it. This can be as simple as a bow of the head with a thank you to all seen and unseen with the understanding that there is gratitude on everyone's behalf for this work. Sometimes a lengthier closing is needed which is accomplished by a bow of the head and torso held for several minutes until the feeling of completion arises.

Chapter Five: General Exercises

Tonight, I am listening to a deeper way. Suddenly, all my ancestors are behind me. "Be still," they say. "Watch and listen. You are the result of the love of thousands."[14]

Your Parents

Assessing the connection and love available to us through our parents is the fundamental building block of Family Energetics. This exercise will introduce you to feeling into this connection, noticing what exists, and releasing some of the emotions around these connections. Please note that while valuable information is in your response, and it is okay to be aware of those thoughts, do not get attached to the idea that those thoughts are the truth. Notice, dig deeper, and let it flow.

When to Use

- You do not know the specific events in your family history.
- You want to start the work from an intuitive gestalt perspective.
- You want to assess where you are with respect to the flow of family love.

---

[14] Linda Hogan, *Dwellings: A Spiritual History of the Living World* (New York: Touchstone, 1996), p. 159.

Chapter Five

Setting the Stage
Imagine you are facing your parents. Imagine your parents not as a certain age or looking a certain way. Instead, connect to the essence of who they are, the sum of all their actions, beliefs and ages. If you need to separate them and do one at a time, that exercise follows after this one. Illustration 5 below shows the general set-up of you and your parents.

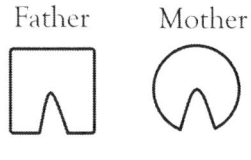

Illustration 5: Facing Your Parents

Sensing the Field
As you face your parents together, take a deep breath and notice what is happening. Be deliberate and thoughtful and gentle with each question. We are witnessing something precious and touched with grace as we look at this relationship.

- Is your energy drawn more to one parent than the other?

- How do you feel when you look at your father?

- How do you feel when you look at your mother?

- Can you imagine them standing close to each other?

- Or are they at a distance from each other?
- Are they looking at you?
- Can you look at them?
- Do you feel incomplete?
- Or do you feel at ease?
- Do you feel they are available?
- Are they distracted by something or someone else?
- Do you feel the love that created you?
- Is there tension in your body?
- Where do you feel it?
- What are the thoughts that go with the tension? Thoughts like:
    - They do not love me.
    - They are not available for me.
    - They do not get me.
    - I miss them.
    - I never got what I needed.

0__1__2__3__4__5__6__7__8__9__10

Connection Between You and Your Parents

Rate your current response on a scale from zero to ten. Zero is you feel no connection at all or you feel intense sadness and loss. Ten is a sense of connection, ease, flow, relief, and love.

Reiterative Tapping for Tension with Both Parents

After assessing how you feel when you face your parents, I invite you to the following tapping. Tap on the karate chop points while saying:

Even though I feel this tension in my body when I look at my parents, I feel this ache, this loss, I deeply and completely love and accept myself.

Even though I feel this tension in my body when I look at my parents, I feel this ache, this loss, I deeply and completely love and accept myself.

Even though I feel this tension in my body when I look at my parents, I feel this ache, this loss, I deeply and completely love and accept myself.

Move through the points using the following phrases, using one phrase per round.

1. This tension.
2. This longing.
3. This ache.
4. This desire to connect.

The first round of tapping is:

1. Tap on the eyebrow about seven times while saying "this tension".

2. Then tap on the side of the eye while saying "this tension".

3. Then tap under the eye while saying "this tension".

4. Then tap the under the nose point while saying "this tension".

5. Then tap the chin point while saying "this tension".

6. Then tap on the collarbone while saying "this tension".

7. Then tap under the arm while saying "this tension".

8. Finally, tap on the crown of the head saying "this tension".

This is one round of tapping. You would then repeat the sequence of the eight points while saying "this longing" for another round.

1. Tap on the eyebrow about seven times while saying "this longing".

2. Then tap on the side of the eye while saying "this longing".

3. Then tap under the eye while saying "this longing".

4. Then tap the under the nose point while saying "this longing".

5. Then tap the chin point while saying "this longing".

6. Then tap on the collarbone while saying "this longing".

7. Then tap under the arm while saying "this longing".

Chapter Five

8. Finally, tap on the crown of the head saying "this longing".

This is the second round of tapping using the second phrase. The third round of tapping is using the phrase "this ache".

1. Tap on the eyebrow about seven times while saying "this ache".

2. Then tap on the side of the eye while saying "this ache".

3. Then tap under the eye while saying "this ache".

4. Then tap the under the nose point while saying "this ache".

5. Then tap the chin point while saying "this ache".

6. Then tap on the collarbone while saying "this ache".

7. Then tap under the arm while saying "this ache".

8. Finally, tap on the crown of the head saying "this ache".

The final round of tapping this time is using the phrase "this desire to connect".

1. Tap on the eyebrow about seven times while saying "this desire to connect".

2. Then tap on the side of the eye while saying "this desire to connect".

3. Then tap under the eye while saying "this desire to connect".

General Exercises

4. Then tap on the under the nose point while saying "this desire to connect".

5. Then tap the chin point while saying "this desire to connect".

6. Then tap on the collarbone while saying "this desire to connect".

7. Then tap under the arm while saying "this desire to connect".

8. Finally, tap on the crown of the head saying "this desire to connect".

Cascading Tapping for Tension with Both Parents
Tapping on the karate chop points, say the following:

Even though I feel this tension in my body when I look at my parents, I feel this ache, this loss, I love and accept myself anyway.

Even though I feel this longing in my body, I want it gone, I am open to the idea of honoring my desire for connection.

Even though I cannot imagine feeling at peace with my parents, I am open to the idea of accepting the fact that they are indeed my parents.

Moving through the points, tapping each point about five to seven times, say the phrases in order:

Eyebrow: This tension.

Side of the Eye: This longing.

Under the Eye: This love.

Under the Nose: This ache.

Chin: This sense of loss.

Collarbone: I honor my desire for connection.

Under the Arm: I honor my desire for my parents.

Head: I honor my desire for love.

Eyebrow: These are my parents.

Side of the Eye: They do not feel available to me.

Under the Eye: They are not available.

Under the Nose: Something is distracting them.

Chin: I am open to seeing the bigger picture.

Collarbone: I am open to seeing the love flowing in the wrong direction.

Under the Arm: I am open to seeing the love flowing in the right direction.

Head: I am open to taking my place in this world.

Intuited Tapping for Tension with Both Parents
Do about three rounds of tapping using your own language inspired by what you notice or have read. Use what you feel physically and emotionally and notice what thoughts occur to you.

Close the Exercise
Choose one of the following to close the exercise.

- Bow your head with a thank you to all seen and unseen.

- Bow the head and torso held for several minutes until the feeling of completion arises.

- Place your hands to the heart with a bow of the head.

- Complete a symbolic physical and energetic closing of your own design.

The Healing Picture
This exercise is working when:

- You notice a shift in the feeling of connection.

- You have an idea of where to work next in the matrix.

- You feel appreciation for the one gift parents gave you, life. Anything above and beyond life is merely a bonus.

At this point you are not looking for immediate closure or healing but an opening of connection and perhaps an idea of where to look next. Do a few more rounds if you feel energy moving or new thoughts appearing.

What is Next
If you noticed that the connection to one parent is markedly different than the other parent, you can do this exercise one parent at a time. Otherwise, take a deliberate break, a deep breath, a stretch, or a drink. Or even sleep on it and come back tomorrow for the grandparents' piece of this.

Chapter Five

Your Mother

Setting the Stage

Face your biological mother whether she is dead or alive, known or unknown. Do not imagine her at any specific age; rather just sense her entire being and energy.

Mother

Illustration 6: Facing Mother

Sensing the Field

- How much tension do you feel in your body?

- How much ease do you feel?

- Do you smile with recognition?

- Do you freeze with uncertainty?

- Do you feel unnamed sadness?

- Where do you feel the tension?

- What thoughts go with the tension? Thoughts like:
  - She does not love me.
  - She isn't available for me.
  - She does not get me.
  - I miss her.
  - I never got what I needed.

Rate your current connection on a scale from zero to ten. Zero is no connection at all, with intense sadness and sense of loss. Ten is ease, flow, relief, and love.

0__1__2__3__4__5__6__7__8__9__10

Connection Between You and Your Mother

Reiterative Tapping for Longing and Disconnection with Your Mother

Tap on the karate chop points while saying the following:

Even though I feel this longing and this disconnection, I love and accept myself just as I am.

Even though I feel this longing and this disconnection, I love and accept myself just as I am.

Even though I feel this longing and this disconnection, I love and accept myself just as I am.

Tap one round of points for each expression for a total of three rounds.

1. This disconnection with my mother.
2. This desire to feel the love she gave me.
3. She gave me life and the rest I got elsewhere.

Finish with the karate chop points:

Even though I do not understand, I am open to seeing more.

Even though I do not understand, I am open to taking my place.

Even though I do not understand, I acknowledge the desire for connection and love.

Cascading Tapping

Tapping on the karate chop points, say:

Even though I feel both this love and this longing, I love and accept myself just as I am.

Even though I wish something were different with my mother, I love and accept myself exactly as I am.

Even though I feel regret and tension, something is missing, I love and accept myself exactly as I am.

Moving through the points:

Eyebrow: My mother.

Side of the Eye: I am her child.

Under the Eye: This disconnection.

Under the Nose: All this longing.

Chin: I wish it were different.

Collarbone: I wish I could feel at peace.

Under the Arm: I wish I could feel completely connected.

Head: This longing for connection.

Eyebrow: My mother who gave me life.

Side of the Eye: She does not feel available to me.

Under the Eye: She is tied up in the past.

Under the Nose: She does it out of loyalty for the family.

Chin: I wish it were different.

Collarbone: I wish I could feel the love.

Under the Arm: I am open to seeing what is.

Head: I am open to seeing what happened.

Back to karate chop points:

Even though I do not understand, I am open to seeing more.

Even though I do not understand, I am open to taking my place.

Even though I do not understand, I acknowledge the desire for connection and love.

Intuited Tapping
Do about three rounds of tapping using your own language inspired by what you notice or have read. Use what you feel

physically and emotionally. Notice what thoughts occur to you as you tap.

Close the Exercise

An expression of closure and gratitude is appropriate after every exercise. This might include one of the following:

- Bowing your head with a thank you to all seen and unseen.

- Bowing your head and torso held for several minutes until the feeling of completion arises.

- Placing your hands to the heart with a bow of the head.

- Choosing a symbolic physical and energetic closing of your own design.

What is Next

Now take a deliberate break, a deep breath, a stretch, or a drink. Or sleep on it and come back tomorrow. We will be doing the same exercise for your father and then move on to the grandparents.

Your Father

Setting the Stage
Face your biological father whether he's dead or alive, known or unknown. Do not imagine him at any specific age; rather just sense his entire being and energy.

Illustration 7: Facing Father

Sensing the Field
Notice how much ease or tension you feel in your body.

- Do you smile with recognition?
- Do you freeze with uncertainty?
- Do you feel unnamed sadness?
- If tension exists, where do you feel it?
- What thoughts go with the tension? Thoughts like:
    - He does not love me.

- He isn't available for me.
- He does not get me.
- I miss him.
- I never got what I needed.

Rate your current connection on a scale from zero to ten. Zero is no connection at all, with intense sadness and sense of loss. Ten is ease, flow, relief, and love.

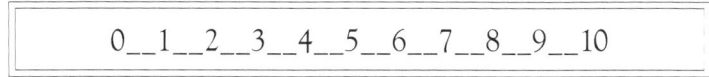

Connection Between You and Your Father

Reiterative Tapping for Longing and Disconnection with Your Father

Tap on the karate chop points while saying the following:

Even though I feel regret and tension, something is missing, I love and accept myself exactly as I am.

Even though I feel regret and tension, something is missing, I love and accept myself exactly as I am.

Even though I feel regret and tension, something is missing, I love and accept myself exactly as I am.

Tap one round for each expression for a total of three rounds.

1. This disconnection with my father.
2. This desire to feel the life he gave me.
3. He gave me life and the rest I got elsewhere.

Finish with the karate chop points:

Even though I do not understand, I am open to seeing more.

Even though I do not understand, I am open to taking my place.

Even though I do not understand, I acknowledge the desire for connection and love.

Cascading Tapping

Tapping on the karate chop points, say:

Even though I feel both this love and this longing, I love and accept myself just as I am.

Even though I wish something were different with my father, I love and accept myself exactly as I am.

Even though I feel regret and tension, something is missing, I love and accept myself exactly as I am.

Moving through the points:

Eyebrow: My father.

Side of the Eye: I am his child.

Under the Eye: All this disconnection.

Under the Nose: All this longing.

Chin: I wish it were different.

Collarbone: I wish I could feel at peace.

Under the Arm: I wish I could feel completely connected.

Chapter Five

Head: This longing for connection.

Back to karate chop points:

Even though I do not understand, I am open to seeing more.

Even though I do not understand, I am open to taking my place.

Even though I do not understand, I acknowledge the desire for connection and love.

Remember that while valuable information is in your response, and it is okay to notice the thoughts, do not get attached to the idea that those thoughts are the truth. Bow your head in recognition of what is and move to the next step.

Close the Exercise
Choose one of the following to close the exercise.

- Bow your head with a thank you to all seen and unseen.

- Bow the head and torso held for several minutes until the feeling of completion arises.

- Place your hands to the heart with a bow of the head.

- Complete a symbolic physical and energetic closing of your own design.

What is Next
Now take a deliberate break, a deep breath, a stretch, or a drink. Or even sleep on it and come back tomorrow. For the next experience, you will be moving into more of an observer role.

The Previous Generation

A disconnection from our parents is often a disconnection somewhere in the lineage. This following exercise points the way to that gap.

When to Use

- After doing the parental portion of this exercise.
- You do not know the specific events in your family history.
- You want to continue the work from an intuitive gestalt perspective.

Your Father's Line

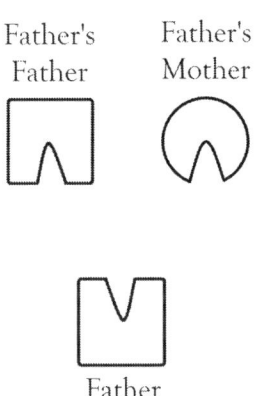

Illustration 8: Your Father Facing His Parents

Chapter Five

Setting the Stage

Imagine your father facing his parents. You are now just a bystander observing.

Sensing the Field

- What do you notice in the energy of your father?
- What do you notice in the energy of your grandmother and grandfather?
- What do you notice between your grandparents?
- What do you notice **between** your father and his parents?
- Do you notice sadness?
- Do you notice delight?
- Are you aware of a feeling of closeness? Or do you notice distance?
- Does longing appear?
- Can you notice the love?
- How big is the gap between them?

0__1__2__3__4__5__6__7__8__9__10

Connection Between Your Father and His Parents

Mark on the scale the level of connection you feel between your father and his parents. Zero is no connection at all with a sense of unease and flatness. Ten is connected, loving and engaged.

Your Mother's Line

Setting the Stage

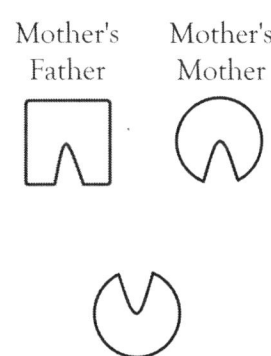

Illustration 9: Your Mother Facing Her Parents

Imagine your mother facing her parents.

Sensing the Field
- What do you notice in the energy of your mother?
- What do you notice in the energy of your grandmother and grandfather?
- What do you notice between your grandparents?

Chapter Five

- What do you notice **between** your mother and her parents?
- Are you aware of sadness?
- Do you notice feelings of delight?
- Do you feel their closeness?
- Or do you notice distance?
- Does longing show between them?
- Does love appear?
- How big is the gap between them?

Mark on the scale that follows the level of connection you feel between your mother and her parents. Zero is no connection at all with a sense of unease and flatness. Ten is connected, loving and engaged.

0__1__2__3__4__5__6__7__8__9__10

Connection Between Your Mother and Her Parents

Next Step

Pick the parent who holds the most tension with their parents and now focus on that set of grandparents and their parents, your great-grandparents.

Grandparents

Setting the Stage
For this next exercise, choose the parent where you notice the most tension in the previous exercise. We will work first with the mother of that parent, your grandmother. Imagine this grandmother facing her parents, your great-grandparents. Remember, this is the mother of whichever parent held the most tension in the previous exercise.

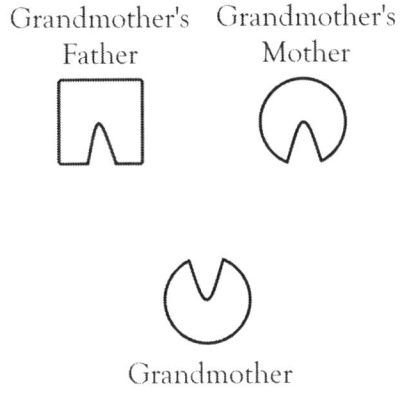

Sensing the Field
- What do you notice in the energy of your grandmother?

- What do you notice in the energy of your great-grandmother and great-grandfather?

- What do you notice between your great-grandparents?

Chapter Five

- What do you notice **between** your grandmother and her parents?
- Is sadness present?
- Are you aware of delight?
- Do you notice closeness?
- Is the distance close or far between them?
- Do you feel a sense of longing?
- Is the love available or observable?
- How big is the gap between them?

Mark on the scale that follows the level of connection you feel between your grandmother and her parents. Zero is no connection at all with a sense of unease and flatness. Ten is connected, loving and engaged.

0__1__2__3__4__5__6__7__8__9__10

Connection Between Grandmother and Her Parents

Setting the Stage

We will work now with the father of the parent that held the most tension in the Previous Generation exercise. Imagine this grandfather facing his parents, your great-grandparents. Remember, this grandfather is the father of the parent that held the most tension.

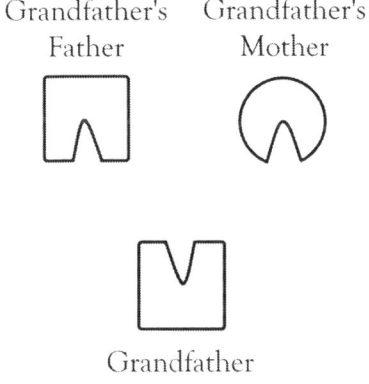

Sensing the Field

- What do you notice in the energy of your grandfather?

- What do you notice in the energy of your great-grandmother and great-grandfather?

- What do you notice between your great-grandparents?

- What do you notice **between** your grandfather and his parents?

- Do you notice any sadness?

Chapter Five

- Do you notice any anger?
- Do you notice a feeling of closeness?
- Or it is more a sense of distance?
- Are you aware of a sense of longing?
- How easily does the love flow?
- How big is the gap between them?

Mark on the scale that follows the level of connection you feel between your grandfather and his parents. Zero is no connection at all with a sense of unease and flatness. Ten is connected, loving and engaged.

0__1__2__3__4__5__6__7__8__9__10

Connection Between Grandfather and His Parents

Disconnection in Family Lineage

When to Use
For any of the grandparent to great-grandparent relationships that feel strained in the previous assessment, please move on to the tapping that follows.

Reiterative Tapping
While tapping the karate chop points, say:

Even though I feel this disconnection in my family, I can feel the tension between generations and I am paying the price, I love and accept myself completely.

Even though I feel this disconnection in my family, I can feel the tension between generations and I am paying the price, I love and accept myself completely.

Even though I feel this disconnection in my family, I can feel the tension between generations and I am paying the price, I love and accept myself completely.

Moving through the points, tap one round for each phrase for a total of six rounds.

1. This painful disconnection and tension.
2. My heart aches.
3. My body constricts.
4. I want my family to feel whole again.
5. I want my family to feel complete again.

Chapter Five

6. I want my family to reconnect.

Cascading Tapping

Tapping on the karate chop points, say:

Even though I feel this disconnection in my family, I can feel the tension between generations and I am paying the price, I love and accept myself completely.

Even though I can feel this disconnection in my family, and while it is affecting me, it is not personal, it is not my fault, I love and accept myself completely.

Even though I can feel this disconnection, and I do not understand the reason why, I am willing to look with love and honor for all, with an open-mind, and see where the love has gotten stuck.

Eyebrow: This painful disconnection.

Side of the Eye: This painful tension.

Under the Eye: This painful constriction.

Under the Nose: My heart aches.

Chin: My heart feels the tension.

Collarbone: My heart feels the constriction.

Under the Arm: I want to know how to feel relief.

Head: I want to know what is needed for my family to feel whole again.

Eyebrow: I want to know what is needed for my family to feel complete again.

Side of the Eye: I want my family to be reconnected.

Under the Eye: I look with loving eyes at my family's past.

Under the Nose: I look with curious eyes at my family's past.

Chin: I look with loving eyes at where the love went astray.

Collarbone: This pain can turn to relief.

Under the Arm: This constriction shows me how much I want to love.

Head: This shows me how much my family wants to love.

Intuited Tapping
Use your own words as you tap on this family line. Look for where your heart freezes when you think of a particular family event or member. As you tap, see what insights occur about why the love got constricted.

Close the Exercise
Choose one of the following to close the exercise.

- Bow your head with a thank you to all seen and unseen.

- Bow the head and torso held for several minutes until the feeling of completion arises.

- Place your hands to the heart with a bow of the head.

- Complete a symbolic physical and energetic closing of your own design.

The Healing Picture
- You feel more at peace with the extended generations.

- You have some insight or compassion for what happened with them.
- You feel some distance from their issues.
- You know you are not to blame.

What is Next

Move on to specific tapping scripts for situations that came up in your family.

Chapter Six: Working with Specifics

Many of my clients have done extensive work on their family of origin. This work often involves clearing childhood trauma and re-parenting themselves in areas that were not fully formed growing up. Mirroring, honoring, and accepting all the parts disowned by the process of growing up are primary components of personal growth and maturation.

Often an unspoken, and sometimes spoken, disowning and distancing from the family of origin occurs. Folks might feel failed by their parents or resigned to leaving their family of origin "behind" so to speak.

This state is not complete healing. We need to look deeper and see what is happening in the larger family system. And indeed, when we look at why the parents were the way they were, what happened before them, what happened to them, we start to see the full picture. We begin to see why the parent/child relationship was sub-optimized at the expense of the child for the *benefit of the whole family system.*

When we see the impacts of our grandparents leaving their homelands and families to come to this country, we can reclaim our entire heritage. When we acknowledge the overlooked child that was aborted, miscarried, or given up, we can be at ease with our current children. When we acknowledge our first loves, see the role the perpetrator has in the system, or see the victims of the wars, we can finally feel at peace in our own bodies, our own lives. You do not have to take my word on this; as you work through the exercises in these chapters, you will come to recognize the acceptance that is possible.

Chapter Six

Where to Start

When we work with the family matrix, we look for unseen, unresolved tension in the system. It is similar to looking for stuck energy in the individual when doing straight EFT. Over time, looking at many constellations, themes or patterns emerge that can lead us to ask questions to reveal the stuck energy.

If doing this work for yourself, make a family history and then start using the tapping scripts for events that fit. If working with clients, ask them about their family history, listening for both emotion and facts. The emotions are a guide to where the energy is stuck. The facts are the clues to what needs to be unraveled. Both emotion and facts must be considered carefully, not held as truth, but rather as signposts to healing.

The following specific questions can help us pinpoint the area to address when working by ourselves or with other individuals.

- How many siblings do you have?
- Did your mother lose any pregnancies?
- Was it your parents' first marriage?
- Did your parents have any lost loves?
- From where did your family emigrate?
- What generation left the other country?
- Do you know of any abortions in the family?

- Who had miscarriages that were known of or suspected?
- Do you know of any adoptions?
- Are other children missing for any reason whatsoever?
- Was anyone involved in a war? What was their role?
- Did anyone die in the war?
- Did anyone suffer a misfortune after coming home from a war?
- Did anyone suffer a misfortune in general?
- Did anyone have a great benefit happen to them?
- Did anyone die early?
- Who got divorced?
- Was anyone considered a war hero?
- Do other heroes exist in the family lore?
- Who was the black sheep?
- Does anyone have a mental illness?
- What unusual events took place in the family history?
- Did sexual abuse or incest occur?
- Did any crimes happen where the family was either the victim or the perpetrator?

Chapter Six

- Did anyone commit or attempt suicide?
- Was anyone raped, whether known or suspected?

You are looking for the following overall themes:

- Who has been excluded in the family history?
- Where has the love been choked off?
- What am I carrying for the family system?

The overall systems thinking principles you are exploring are:

- What is the energy of the entire family system?
- Which relationships are showing strain with the whole system?
- Where am I limited by existing structures such as marriage, divorce, or duty and not seeing the true connections?
- Who is been excluded because I have only looked at immediate relationships?
- What is the path to reconnection?

In the next chapters, you will have a chance to work on specific family situations. If you do not find your particular situation, you can improvise based on the principles discussed in these foundational chapters.

Chapter Seven: Homelands and Loss

He was strong in life. His spirit will find its way to the halls of your fathers.[15]

When We Leave Our Homelands

The United States is known for being somewhat mobile. We move around the country to find work, to go to school, to get married, to follow our dreams, or just to survive. The unspoken price of moving around is leaving our families. In fact, if you look at the energy of the United States as a whole, except for Native Americans, we all left someplace to come here. Other countries world-wide have this same dynamic at various times in their history. Whether our parents, our grandparents, or generations before, many of us chose to leave or were forced to leave.

This hidden loss of our homeland can show up in our lives today as an entanglement. Basically that means that some of our energy is still tied to our ancestors' homelands and until we can see, name, feel, and accept that loss and connection, we will not fully find our places here.

Setting the Stage
Think of your family ancestors. What homelands did they come from? Do you even know? Imagine you are facing your

---

[15] J. R. R. Tolkien, "The Funeral of Theodred," *The Lord of the Rings: The Two Towers*, directed by Peter Jackson (2002; New Line Productions), DVD.

parents; their parents stand behind them with their respective homelands behind them.

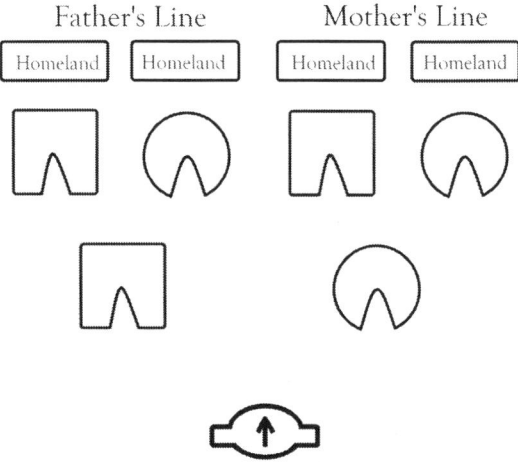

Sensing the Field
Looking at each homeland, one at a time, consider the following.

- Where do you feel loss?
- Where do you feel love?
- Where do you feel disconnected?
- Where do you feel connected?

Face your history and feel the emotion in your body.

Reiterative Tapping
While tapping the karate chop points, say:

Even though our family was split, some of us left and some of us stayed, we still belong to our heritage and homeland.

Even though our family was split, some of us left and some of us stayed, we still belong to our heritage and homeland.

Even though our family was split, some of us left and some of us stayed, we still belong to our heritage and homeland.

Tap one round for each phrase for a total of five rounds.

1. We had to leave.
2. We left our homeland.
3. We left folks behind.
4. We came here to survive, to thrive.
5. We are connected through time and space to our homelands.

Cascading Tapping

While tapping on the set-up points, say:

Even though we left, and we had no choice, we are willing to see what we left behind.

Even though we were glad to leave, we wanted to go, we are willing to see the price we paid.

Even though our family was split, some of us left and some of us stayed, we still belong to our heritage and homeland.

Tap on the designated points while saying the indicated phrase.

Chapter Seven

Eyebrow: I had to leave.

Side of the Eye: We had to leave.

Under the Eye: They had to leave.

Under the Nose: I ignored it.

Chin: I pretended roots do not matter.

Collarbone: I ignored centuries of roots.

Under the Arm: Our homelands have a unique energy.

Head: Our homelands have a unique place in our hearts.

Eyebrow: It is okay to mourn my history.

Side of the Eye: It is okay to claim my history.

Under the Eye: It is okay to see my history.

Under the Nose: It is okay to mourn my ancestral homeland.

Chin: As I accept my family's historical homeland, I can take my place in my current home.

Collarbone: I can love both my ancestor's homeland and my own.

Under the Arm: This loss is also a love.

Head: My ancestors could not see what they left behind.

Eyebrow: My ancestors could not mourn what they lost.

Side of the Eye: They could only look forward.

Under the Eye: But some of them were missing.

Under the Nose: I am willing to honor my past as I look forward.

Chin: I am willing to honor my homeland.

Collarbone: I am willing to honor my ancestors.

Under the Arm: I am willing to take my rightful place in my current home.

Head: I see the past that brought me here.

Intuited Tapping
Tap at least three rounds following your intuited stream of consciousness as it relates to leaving your homelands, the loss, the courage, and the connection that still exists.

Close the Exercise
Choose one of the following to close the exercise.

- Bow your head with a thank you to all seen and unseen.

- Bow the head and torso held for several minutes until the feeling of completion arises.

- Place your hands to the heart with a bow of the head.

- Complete a symbolic physical and energetic closing of your own design.

The Healing Picture
This work is complete when the energy shifts from a hidden loss to a forgotten love to a remembered connection.

Chapter Seven

When We Are Forced to Leave: Enslavement

The most extreme and violent form of leaving our homelands is when people are taken against their will and sold into slavery. If our ancestors were captured from their native countries and sold and enslaved in this country, how do we recognize this, see the loss involved, and reclaim our connection to our past? How do we love our current country?

Substantial healing is needed around the history of slavery in the United States. The Family Constellation world has a rich history with dealing with systemic oppression. John Payne writes of his constellation work addressing apartheid in South Africa. Bert Hellinger's constellation work has a strong connection to Germany where the impact of World War II regularly shows up in constellations. Genocides from other countries' wars often show up in group constellations in the States. Unfortunately, I have seen little work done around the American history of slavery; however, we can do our own work using Family Energetics.

When to Use
When we suspect or know that we have ancestors who were brought here against their will.

Setting the Stage
Imagine seven generations of ancestors standing before you, each row a different generation: your parents, your grandparents, your great-grandparents, your great-great-grandparents, and so on. Seven generations of two people, four people, eight people, sixteen people, 32 people, 64 people, and finally 128 people, a total of 254 people total who came together in their unique way to make you. Feel their

respective homelands behind them, supporting and nourishing them.

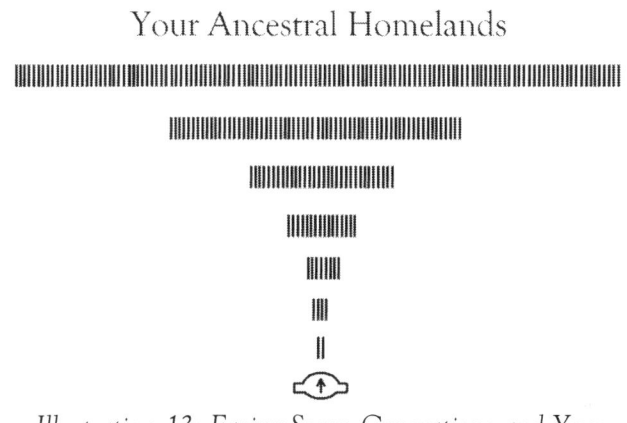

Illustration 13: Facing Seven Generations and Your Ancestral Homelands

Sensing the Field
Taking a deep breath, what do you notice when you see your history in front of you.

- Do you feel anger for a disrupted family?

- Do you notice the pain and loss of being stolen away?

- Do you feel sadness?

- Do you feel connection?

Reiterative Tapping
While tapping the karate chop points, say:

Even though I know this was my history, and it is painful to consider, I am open to seeing what is.

Even though I know this was my history, and it is painful to consider, I am open to seeing what is.

Even though I know this was my history, and it is painful to consider, I am open to seeing what is.

Do one round of tapping for each expression below:

1. Seeing my family history.
2. We were forced to leave our homeland.
3. Being enslaved.
4. The love of my homeland is still with me.

Cascading Tapping

Tapping on the karate chop points, say:

Even though I know this was my history, and it is painful to consider, I am open to seeing what is.

Even though I know my family was enslaved, what I also know is that my family came from {name of homeland}.

Even though my family was enslaved, being enslaved is not our whole story.

Even though my family was stolen from their homeland, I am open to seeing the love of the homeland that is still in our blood.

Tap on the points while saying the phrase shown.

Eyebrow: Seeing my family history.

Side of the Eye: It was not our choice.

Under the Eye: We were made to leave.

Under the Nose: It was not our choice.

Chin: We were forced to leave.

Collarbone: Some of us did not survive.

Under the Arm: The rest of us fought hard to stay alive.

Head: Seeing my family history.

Eyebrow: We were kidnapped and trapped.

Side of the Eye: We were stolen from our homeland and brought here.

Under the Eye: How do we love where we live now when we came here against our will?

Under the Nose: We see and acknowledge our past.

Chin: We honor our homelands.

Collarbone: Our homelands are in our blood.

Under the Arm: We can feel the lineage stretch back across the years and across the waters to our homelands.

Head: We carry the memory of home in our hearts.

Intuited Tapping
Tap at least three rounds following your intuited stream of consciousness as it relates to your ancestors who were enslaved. Do it from a place of connection to your original homeland and the bravery of those who came here.

Close the Exercise
Choose one of the following to close the exercise.

- Bow your head with a thank you to all seen and unseen.

Chapter Seven

- Bow the head and torso held for several minutes until the feeling of completion arises.

- Place your hands to the heart with a bow of the head.

- Complete a symbolic physical and energetic closing of your own design.

The Healing Picture

This exercise is complete when:

- You can feel the lineage through the years back to your homeland.

- You feel pride in where you came from.

- You see being enslaved as a segment of the story but not the whole story.

- You feel the pain and loss and anger but it does not trap you.

War

Humanity is a long way from collectively achieving its full potential of emotional intelligence, but in earlier days we were emotionally retarded, distorted or deeply detached – en masse. How can it be otherwise, considering the constancy of war and brutality, the ubiquitousness of dictatorships, and the careless attitude to our natural environment.[16]

Robin Grille

A bright ambitious woman was launching her own business. She is college educated, resourceful, with clear goals and ambitions, disciplined, intelligent, and knowledgeable in both successful business practices and her field of choice. But she felt that something was holding her back. She could feel it like a physical weight on her back. We did some Family Energetics work and explored the fate of her grandfathers, who both served in World War II and both paid a price for serving.

We looked at the price of being in the war, the lack of choice in joining the war, the loyalty to the country in fighting the war, the anger at the "enemy", the fear, and the isolation. We looked at all the ways the war experience was a weight to her grandfathers. The combination of seeing these issues as well as tapping dramatically shifted her feelings of being held back. **The replacement attitude was of gratitude and moving forward in honor of her grandfathers.**

---

[16] Robin Grille, *Parenting for aPeaceful World,* (New South Wales, Australia: Longueville Media. 2005) p. 94.

Chapter Seven

The theme of war comes up often in my work with clients and in group constellations I have witnessed. Is it any wonder when the personal price of war is so high and the effects so broad? A peace comes from looking and seeing the consequences of our family members' actions and grieving the losses our families experienced during the war. The grandchildren of the tragedies are often the ones who have the strength, love, and distance to look at these events.

When to Use
This exercise can be helpful when:

- You know a family member served in a war.
- You know a family member died in a war.
- You know a family member was injured in a war.
- Your family line was impacted by war in other ways.

Setting the Stage
Think of an ancestor who had to fight in a war. Imagine him standing in front of you at a slight distance and imagine the energy of the war around him. Imagine his victims lying on the floor next to him.[17] If he did not directly kill others but contributed to the death of others, you can still sense the victims lying on the floor.

---

[17] This position on the floor indicates the early or unusual death of someone. We use it in several exercises in this book.

Homelands and Loss

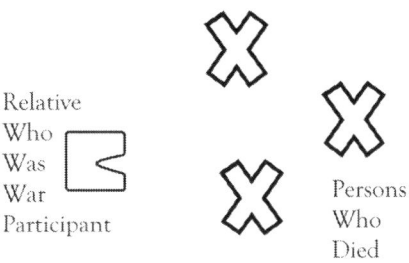

Relative Who Was War Participant

Persons Who Died

Observing From A Distance

Sensing the Field

Notice what you feel for yourself and what you feel in the room. Remember that while these emotions can feel overwhelming and irresolvable, with tapping and the right phrases, they will evolve.

Reiterative Tapping from the Perspective of the One Who Contributed to the Harm of Others

While tapping the karate chop points, say:

Even though I do not want to look at what I did, I am open to the idea of loving and accepting myself.

Even though I do not want to look at what I did, I am open to the idea of loving and accepting myself.

Even though I do not want to look at what I did, I am open to the idea of loving and accepting myself.

Moving through the points, tap one round for each phrase for a total of three rounds.

Chapter Seven

1. I did this out of loyalty; I did this because it was war.
2. The price of war is high.
3. Part of me died when I did this.

Moving back to the set-up points, say the following while tapping on the karate chop points:

Even though I know what I did, I love and accept myself.

Even though I will always carry what I did in my heart, I am open to the idea that I can keep living even while knowing this.

Going back to the points, do another four rounds, one round per phrase.

1. I did this.
2. I choose to see what I did.
3. These persons I hurt, killed, and maimed.
4. I see you.

Cascading Tapping from the Perspective of the One Who Contributed to the Harm of Others

Tapping on the karate chop points, say:

Even though I do not want to look at what I did, I am open to the idea of loving and accepting myself.

Even though I cannot look at what I did, I am open to the idea of loving and accepting myself.

Even though I know what I did, I love and accept myself.

Even though I will always carry what I did in my heart, I am open to the idea that I can keep living even while knowing this.

Eyebrow: I did this out of loyalty.

Side of the Eye: I did this because it was war.

Under the Eye: I did this because it was war.

Under the Nose: I did not want to do this.

Chin: I had to do this.

Collarbone: The price of war is high.

Under the Arm: Part of me died when I did this.

Head: Part of me died when I did this.

Eyebrow: I did this.

Side of the Eye: I cannot look.

Under the Eye: I must look.

Under the Nose: I will look.

Chin: These persons I hurt.

Collarbone: These persons I killed.

Under the Arm: The price of war is high.

Head: I see you now.

Eyebrow: I am willing to see you.

Side of the Eye: It was war.

Under the Eye: And the price of war is high.

Under the Nose: I live with what I did.

Chin: I carry what I did in my heart.

Collarbone: These persons I killed.

Under the Arm: The price of war is high.

Head: I see you now.

Reiterative Tapping from the Wounded or Killed Perspective
While tapping the set-up points, say the following:

Even though my family lost a father, a brother, a son, an uncle, I am willing to grieve this loss.

Even though my family lost a father, a brother, a son, an uncle, I am willing to grieve this loss.

Even though my family lost a father, a brother, a son, an uncle, I am willing to grieve this loss.

Tap one round per expression for a total of five rounds.

1. The loss from the war.
2. My family lost a son, a father, a brother, an uncle.
3. I see you.
4. I see all of you.
5. I see the price we all paid for this war.

Cascading Tapping from the Wounded or Killed Perspective
Even though my family was killed during the war, and it feels personal and ugly and at the same time long ago, I am open to opening my heart to this loss.

Even though my country was crushed by losses, and we were not able to grieve completely, I, as a grandchild, as the next- next generation, am willing to see the price we paid for this war.

Even though my family lost a father, a brother, a son, an uncle, I am willing to grieve this loss.

Even though part of the family died when this person died, I am open to seeing this loss.

Moving though the points:

Eyebrow: Seeing our loss from the war.

Side of the Eye: My family lost a son, a father, a brother, an uncle.

Under the Eye: This loss from the war.

Under the Nose: Our families paid a price.

Chin: Our countries paid a price.

Collarbone: I see you.

Under the Arm: I see all of you.

Head: The price we paid for the war.

Eyebrow: We are bound together by our losses.

Side of the Eye: Both the killed and the killers are connected.

Under the Eye: We were at war.

Under the Nose: We did not want to be here.

Chin: We did it out of loyalty to our countries.

Collarbone: We did it out of fear for our countries.

Under the Arm: We paid with our lives.

Head: I am able to see these losses with love.

Intuited Tapping

Tap at least three rounds following your intuited stream of consciousness as it relates to the loss of the family members in war. Remember that a connection exists between killed and killer, and judgment and indignation only serve to disrupt this connection. Seeing the loss from both perspectives, seeing the difficult decisions, and seeing the loyalties and obligations to the larger country is the key to relief.

Close the Exercise

Choose one of the following to close the exercise.

- Bow your head with a thank you to all seen and unseen.

- Bow the head and torso held for several minutes until the feeling of completion arises.

- Place your hands to the heart with a bow of the head.

- Complete a symbolic physical and energetic closing of your own design.

The Healing Picture

This healing is working when:

- You can look and see peace between the killed and the killer.

- You can see their fate and their strength in accepting and living their fates.

Early or Unexpected Losses

Many family matrix sessions involve unresolved, unseen grief and loss from generations ago. This unseen loss was driven underground and is causing limitations in our lives today. Resolution includes seeing and acknowledging the loss and the people involved. Since we have some distance from the event via time but are still connected through blood and love, we are in the ideal position to bring closure to this event. The grandchildren are often the ones that can do the healing since they are removed enough from the events but are connected enough to remember the pain.

When to Use
This exercise can be helpful when:

- You know of stillborn children in your family history.
- You know of infant deaths.
- You know of accidents resulting in loss of life.
- You know of mothers or fathers dying young.
- You know of siblings dying early.
- You know of lost loves dying young.
- You know of a father or son or child lost at war.
- You know of a mother dying in childbirth.
- Or you might not know any specifics but you have an intuitive sense of loss.

Chapter Seven

Setting the Stage

Imagine, experience, sense, or intuit the person who died too young lying on the floor in front of you. You are not seeing their specific characteristics, just the gestalt of their being. Sense the person who loved him or her standing next to the lost person.

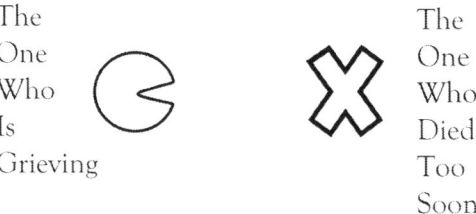

The	The
One	One
Who	Who
Is	Died
Grieving	Too
	Soon

Observing From a Distance

Sensing the Field
- What do you notice?
- Are there feelings of connection and love?
- Are there feelings of distance and not being able to look?
- Who needs to mourn?
- Who needs to live?
- Do you feel tension?
- Do you feel relief?

Now imagine inviting the standing person to kneel down next to the person on the floor. Do this gently and intentionally. Open your heart to the sorrow and grief involved while also maintaining a respectful distance; this is not your sorrow.

Reiterative Tapping for the Griever
While tapping the karate chop points, say:

Even though you died too young, and we miss you, we claim our love for you.

Even though you died too young, and we miss you, we claim our love for you.

Even though you died too young, and we miss you, we claim our love for you.

Do one round of tapping for each expression for a total of three rounds.

1. You left too soon.
2. We needed you.
3. You will always have a place in our hearts.

Back to the set-up points:

Even though part of me died when you died, I see the love we share.

Even though part of me died when you died, I see the love we share.

Do one round of tapping for each expression for a total of two rounds.

1. Part of me died when you died.

Chapter Seven

    2. I want to stay with you.

Even though it is not my time to come, I see the love we share.

Do one round of tapping on each expression for a total of three rounds.

    1. It is not my time yet.

    2. I chose to stay.

    3. You will always be in my heart.

Cascading Tapping

Tapping on the karate chop points, say:

Even though I lost you and I cannot grieve you yet, I am open to seeing my feelings.

Even though you died too young, and I miss you, I am open to claiming my love for you.

Even though I lost you and I miss you, I am open to accepting my feelings.

Moving through the points:

Eyebrow: You left too soon.

Side of the Eye: You left too soon.

Under the Eye: Part of me wants to be with you.

Under the Nose: All of me wants to be with you.

Chin: You left too soon.

Collarbone: We needed you.

Under the Arm: I needed you.

Head: You left too soon.

Back to the karate chop points:

Even though part of me wants to be with you, I love and accept my feelings.

Even though part of me is with you, I accept my choices.

Even though part of me needs to be with you, I love and accept myself.

Moving through the points again:

Eyebrow: Part of me died when you died.

Side of the Eye: This sorrow.

Under the Eye: This grief.

Under the Nose: Part of me died when you died.

Chin: This grief.

Collarbone: This sorrow.

Under the Arm: This loss.

Head: Part of me died when you died.

Back to the set-up points:

Even though the rest of the family needs me, I am open to the conflict I feel.

Even though it is not my time to come, I am open to wanting to be with you.

Moving through the rounds:

Eyebrow: It is not my time yet.

Side of the Eye: I choose to stay.

Under the Eye: It is not my time yet.

Under the Nose: I choose to stay.

Chin: I see you.

Collarbone: You will always be in my heart.

Under the Arm: I see you.

Head: You will always be in our hearts.

Intuited Tapping

Tap at least three rounds following your intuited stream of consciousness as it relates to this loss. Acknowledge both the desire to collapse and stay with the lost person as well as the pull towards life.

Close the Exercise

Choose one of the following to close the exercise.

- Bow your head with a thank you to all seen and unseen.

- Bow the head and torso held for several minutes until the feeling of completion arises.

- Place your hands to the heart with a bow of the head.

- Complete a symbolic physical and energetic closing of your own design.

The Healing Picture

This exercise is done when:

- You see the person who died too young and can feel some peace.

- You see how much he or she was loved.

- You see the heart-based connection between who died and who lived.

Chapter Seven

Family Lore, Unusual Events, Crimes, and Black Sheep

Each family has its own oral tradition and history with stories of good deeds and bad, losses and gains, good guys and villains.

1. Take a few minutes and see what family stories come to mind for you and your history. Try to list at least three.

2. See if you notice a theme with the stories. A theme of leaving and loss might be apparent. Or financial fortunes and failures. Or children lost at every generation.

3. Make a note of what you tell yourself based on these stories. Be as honest as you can and listen to the unnamed family loyalties that might be at play here.

4. Now let us look at this from a Family Energetics point of view.

When to Use
This exercise can be helpful when:

- You notice family stories that feel restrictive.
- You are aware of family lore that has never been questioned.
- You have a sense of a family fate that cannot be escaped.

Setting the Stage
Imagine all the main characters of your family stories standing in front of you. Include both the person who did the action and the person who might have suffered. I did not include an illustration for this exercise because each situation is unique and I do not know how many people are in your exercise. By now I hope that you have an idea of how to create the set-up. You might want to draw a diagram of the people involved.

Sensing the Field
- What do you notice?
- What is the energy flow between participants?
- How is the energy of each family member?
- Who feels connected and available?
- Who feels cut-off or restricted?
- Are there any new aspects that show up for you?
- Does anyone else need to be included?

Reiterative Tapping
Tapping on the karate chop points, say the following to each person in the picture:

Even though I have felt incomplete because I cannot see the whole story, I am open to seeing the love in your actions.

Even though I have felt incomplete because I cannot see the whole story, I am open to seeing the love in your actions.

Even though I have felt incomplete because I cannot see the whole story, I am open to seeing the love in your actions.

Tap one round for each expression for a total of four rounds.

1. I acknowledge what you did for love and for life.
2. I acknowledge the cost to you.
3. I acknowledge the benefit to you.
4. I acknowledge what others gained and lost.

Cascading Tapping

Tapping on the karate chop points, say:

Even though I do not know the whole story, I am open to the idea that you did what you had to do.

Even though I do not know your whole story, I am open to seeing that you lived with the consequences of what you did.

Even though I have felt incomplete because I cannot see the whole story, I am open to seeing the price and the benefit of your actions.

Moving through the points:

Eyebrow: I acknowledge what you did for love.

Side of the Eye: I acknowledge what you did for life.

Under the Eye: I acknowledge the cost to you.

Chin: I acknowledge the benefit to you.

Collarbone: I acknowledge what others gained.

Under the Arm: I acknowledge what others lost.

Head: I leave this with you with love and respect. It is not mine.

Intuited Tapping
Keeping love and openness as the underlying themes, tap at least three rounds following your intuited stream of consciousness.

Close the Exercise
Choose one of the following to close the exercise.

- Bow your head with a thank you to all seen and unseen.

- Bow the head and torso held for several minutes until the feeling of completion arises.

- Place your hands to the heart with a bow of the head.

- Complete a symbolic physical and energetic closing of your own design.

The Healing Picture
This exercise has done its work when:

- You see that this person lived with the consequences.

- You see anyone who suffered as being included.

- You see the larger picture and feel at peace.

- You start to shift your thinking and experience of the story and see other possibilities for what happened.

Chapter Eight: Love and Loss

Every romantic relationship we have had in the past either contributes to or takes away from our current relationship. Contrary to popular relationship advice, it is not a matter of letting go of the past; it is a matter of honoring our past partners and acknowledging their order so that our current or future loves can be seen and respected as well. By now you might have noticed that "place" is a foundational concept in the field of Family Constellations and Family Energetics. By place, I mean acknowledging the proper order of people and relations with respect to age, relationship, and time.

For partner work, acknowledging the order means being crystal clear that Person A was my first partner, Person B was my second, and Person C is my third. It is not judgment or opinion; it is fact. This is the order.

With all these relationships, you may be feeling self-judgment, blame, shame, anger, or sadness. These feelings limit us in seeing all of our partners in their appropriate place and will cause us problems in our current relationships.

As we use our intuition to see if disruption exists in the field around our partners, we can use specific healing phrases and tapping to clear the field. Yes, your former and current partners are permanent members of your family matrix.

Chapter Eight

First Loves

Our first loves have a huge impact on our hearts; whether it was the first person with whom we were physically intimate, our first high school crush, or our first marriage, honoring our first loves and taking responsibility for our contribution to the relationship is pivotal to being available in later relationships.

When to Use
I pretty much recommend this exercise for everyone. In particular this exercise can be helpful if:

- You feel regret for your first partner.
- You feel resentment for your first partner.
- You feel unresolved longing for your first partner.

Setting the Stage
Think of who your first love is. The definition might vary for each person but you will know. If the person was your first consensual sexual experience but not true love, still consider him or her your first partner.

Sensing the Field
Sense this person standing in front of you. Imagine looking into her or his eyes and see what you feel and notice.

Or if your first love were female:

Illustration 17: First Love Female

Reiterative Tapping
While tapping on the set-up points, say:

Even though you were my first, and I feel sadness, love, anger (note: only use words that fit your experience), *I acknowledge you as my first.*

Even though you were my first, and I feel sadness, love, anger (note: only use words that fit your experience), *I acknowledge you as my first.*

Even though you were my first, and I feel sadness, love, anger (note: only use words that fit your experience), *I acknowledge you as my first.*

Tap one round for each expression for a total of five rounds.

1. With all that it cost me and all that it cost you, you were my first.
2. With all that it gave me and all that it gave you, you were my first.
3. I take responsibility for my part as you take responsibility for your part.
4. I am open to seeing the love we had together.
5. Wish me well as I am now available for another as I wish you well as you are available for another.

Cascading Tapping

Tapping on the karate chop points, say:

Even though you were my first, and I feel sadness, love, anger (note: only use words that fit your experience), *I am open to seeing you as my first.*

Even though I have moved on, part of me never did move on, and I acknowledge both parts of me.

Even though I did not know what to do with my feelings for you, both good and bad, I am open to seeing the love we had together.

Moving through the points:

Eyebrow: You were my first.

Side of the Eye: With all that it cost me and all that it cost you, you were my first.

Under Eye: You were my first.

Under the Nose: With all that it gave me and all that it gave you, you were my first.

Chin: You were my first.

Collarbone: With all that it gave us and all that it cost us, you were my first.

Under the Arm: I take responsibility for my part as you take responsibility for your part.

Head: I take responsibility for my part as you take responsibility for your part.

Eyebrow: I am open to seeing that I was available to you.

Side of Eye: I am open to seeing that I was NOT available to you.

Under Eye: I am open to seeing the affection between us.

Under the Nose: I am open to seeing what we gave each other.

Chin: I am open to seeing how we fit each other.

Collarbone: Thank you.

Underarm: Wish me well as I am available for another.

Head: I wish you well as you are available for another.

Intuited Tapping

Tap at least three rounds following your intuited stream of consciousness as it relates to how you feel about realizing your first love and his/her place in your life. Look at it without blame or judgment, just accepting and seeing what was, what is, and what might be.

Close the Exercise

Choose one of the following to close the exercise.

- Bow your head with a thank you to all seen and unseen.

- Bow the head and torso held for several minutes until the feeling of completion arises.

- Place your hands to the heart with a bow of the head.

- Complete a symbolic physical and energetic closing of your own design.

The Healing Picture

This exercise is working when:

- You can look at your partner with a sense of ease.

- You feel free of any resentment or lingering emotions.

- You feel available for a current relationship.

Later Partners

For each subsequent relationship, we will do a similar process to the first love tapping but this time we add in the element of place.

When to Use

Again, I pretty much recommend this exercise for everyone. In particular this exercise can be helpful if:

- You are having trouble with existing relationships.
- You are entering a significant new relationship.
- You feel limited by your romantic history.
- You feel unresolved longing, resentment, anger, or grief for any past partner.

Setting the Stage

For this exercise, imagine facing your first, second, and third partners. You will want to do this exercise for all the primary partner relationships you have had.

Chapter Eight

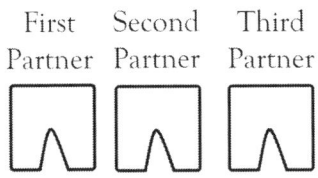

Illustration 18: Facing Former Partners

Sensing the Field

Take a deep breath and imagine looking at each of your partners.

- How does it feel to see each one?
- How does it feel to see all of them together?
- How does it feel to see the history of your love life?
- Do you feel light?
- Do you feel love?
- Do you feel inclusion?
- Do you feel grief?
- Do you feel heaviness?
- Do you feel regret?

Reiterative Tapping

Imagine looking at the second partner while being aware of the first one and tap on the karate chop points:

Even though you were my second, and this was my first, I am open to seeing you both.

Even though you were my second, and this was my first, I am open to seeing you both.

Even though you were my second, and this was my first, I am open to seeing you both.

Tap one round for each phrase for a total of three rounds.

1. You were my second partner, this was my first.
2. My experience with him/her leads to my experience with you.
3. I take responsibility for my part as you take responsibility for your part.

Cascading Tapping

Tapping on the karate chop points, say while looking at the second partner:

Even though you were my second, and this was my first, I am open to seeing you both.

Even though I feel these feelings, I am open to seeing your place in my life.

Even though you were my second, and this was my first, I am open to seeing you both.

Moving through the points:

Eyebrow: You are my second partner.

Side of Eye: This is my first.

Under the Eye: You are my second.

Under the Nose: This is my first.

Chin: My experience with him/her leads to my experience with you.

Collarbone: He came first, you came second.

Under the Arm: You were my second.

Head: I take responsibility for my part.

Eyebrow: You take responsibility for your part.

Side of Eye: You were my second.

Under the Eye: This is my first.

Under the Nose: I see the love we had together.

Chin: I see what we gave each other.

Collarbone: I see what we cost each other.

Under the Arm: Wish me well as I am now available for another.

Head: I wish you well as you are available for another.

Close the Exercise
Choose one of the following to close the exercise.

- Bow your head with a thank you to all seen and unseen.

- Bow the head and torso held for several minutes until the feeling of completion arises.

- Place your hands to the heart with a bow of the head.

- Complete a symbolic physical and energetic closing of your own design.

The Healing Picture

This exercise is done when:

- You can look at your partners with a sense of ease.

- You see how the flow of partners led you to where you are today.

- You claim them all.

Chapter Eight

Divorce

Whether we are the adults getting divorced, the young children of the divorced parents, or even the adult children of divorced parents, divorce matters.

Obviously for the adults getting divorced, there might be feelings of guilt, relief, and grief all mixed up together. For the children, a hidden feeling of not being wanted can linger in their hearts causing damage and pain. Even if the divorce was for the best, and the parents are attentive and supportive, there remains a hidden message that the marriage was a mistake. And if the marriage was a mistake, then the children are a mistake – or at least, that is how they feel.

Conscious attention is needed to reinforce that the children are a product of love, even if the parents cannot stand each other. Seeing the love that created the children even if the relationship is over is the direction of healing.

When to Use
- Whenever there is a divorce in the family involving children.
- If you were the child of divorce.
- If divorce affected your parents.

Setting the Stage
Imagine facing your child(ren) with your former partner next to you. Adjust the illustration that follows to represent all your children in order.

Love and Loss

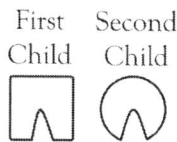

 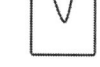

You and Former Partner
As Parents

Illustration 19: You, the Other Parent, and Your Children

Sensing the Field
Notice the energy between all of you.

- Do you notice longing?
- Do you notice loss?
- Do you notice love?
- Do you feel tension?
- Do you feel relief?

Reiterative Tapping
While tapping the karate chop points, say:

Even though the love between me and their father/mother has gone, I see the love that is within our children.

Even though the love between me and their father/mother has gone, I see the love that is within our children.

Even though the love between me and their father/mother has gone, I see the love that is within our children.

Do one round per expression for a total of three rounds.

1. My children are part of us both.
2. I see the love that created the children.
3. I see our love in them.

Cascading Tapping

Tapping on the karate chop points, say:

Even though I do not want to look at my "ex", I accept his/her place as the children's other parent.

Even though when I look at my children I feel love which is not what I feel when I see my former partner, I accept both feelings.

Even though the love between me and their father/mother has gone, I see the love that is within our children.

Eyebrow: My children are part me and part my "ex".

Side of the Eye: Our children come from both of us.

Under the Eye: The marriage is over.

Under the Nose: The love that created the children still lives in them.

Chin: When I look at my children, I see the love we had together.

Collarbone: Our marriage is over.

Under the Arm: The love is over.

Head: The love in our children lives on.

Intuited Tapping

Tap at least three rounds following your intuited stream of consciousness as it relates to the love that created your children.

Close the Exercise

Choose one of the following to close the exercise.

- Bow your head with a thank you to all seen and unseen.

- Bow the head and torso held for several minutes until the feeling of completion arises.

- Place your hands to the heart with a bow of the head.

- Complete a symbolic physical and energetic closing of your own design.

The Healing Picture

This experience has done its work when:

- You see the love that was.

- You acknowledge the place of your former spouse in the creation of your child.

Chapter Eight

Children from New Relationships

The impact of divorce on children continues if one or both of the parents have children with a new partner. Once a new relationship is created through the birth of a child, the newer children take precedence with the parents. The fate of both sets of children can be challenging. The children from the first relationship see what they lost when the new child is born. And the younger children can be at the receiving end of some emotional tension that is not their fault or doing.

Seeing the order of things can free us from the turmoil we feel.

Reiterative Tapping for the Children of the First Relationship
While tapping the karate chop points, say:

Even though I feel like I lost my place in my family when the next child was born, I am open to seeing and grieving this loss.

Even though I feel like I lost my place in my family when the next child was born, I am open to seeing and grieving this loss.

Even though I feel like I lost my place in my family when the next child was born, I am open to seeing and grieving this loss.

Tap one round per expression:

1. I have lost the safety of my mother and father being together.
2. I came first and now a new child needs her family.
3. We both have our places in the new order.

Cascading Tapping
Tapping on the karate chop points, say:

Even though my sibling took my place, and I do not like saying that, I love and accept myself deeply and completely.

Even though I lost my place in my family when they separated, I am open to grieving this loss.

Even though it is not her fault and it is not my fault, I am open to seeing both of our places.

Eyebrow: My sibling took my place.

Side of the Eye: I lost my place when my parents separated.

Under the Eye: My sibling took my place.

Under the Nose: I lost my place when she was born.

Chin: My mother lost her place.

Collarbone: It is a loss for all of us.

Under the Arm: And it is not my sibling's fault.

Head: I lost my place.

Eyebrow: We tried to pretend it did not matter.

Side of the Eye: We tried to pretend it was all the same.

Under the Eye: My mother lost her place.

Under the Nose: I lost my place.

Chin: That is the way it was.

Collarbone: I came first.

Under the Arm: She came second.

Head: I am innocent; so is she.

Intuited Tapping

Tap at least three rounds following your intuited stream of consciousness as it relates to the loss of your place, the innocence of all the children, and seeing the places of everyone in the family.

Close the Exercise

Choose one of the following to close the exercise.

- Bow your head with a thank you to all seen and unseen.

- Bow the head and torso held for several minutes until the feeling of completion arises.

- Place your hands to the heart with a bow of the head.

- Complete a symbolic physical and energetic closing of your own design.

The Healing Picture

This work is complete when:

- You feel a sense of place.

- You recognize the other family that came after you.

- You see the love between your parents that created you.

Love and Loss

Reiterative Tapping for the Younger Child(ren)
While tapping the karate chop points, say:

Even though my gain was another's loss, I am open to seeing my place in the family.

Even though my gain was another's loss, I am open to seeing my place in the family.

Even though my gain was another's loss, I am open to seeing my place in the family.

Do one round for each expression for a total of three rounds.

1. I was not first.
2. I accept the order that is.
3. It is my parents' business, not mine.

Cascading Tapping
Tapping on the karate chop points, say:

Even though I did not choose my place, I am open to seeing what came before me.

Even though I am innocent, I am open to seeing the losses that came before me.

Even though my gain was another's loss, I am open to seeing my place in the family.

Even though I also had a loss by not being the first, I am open to seeing my place in the family.

Moving through the points:

Eyebrow: I was not first.

Chapter Eight

Side of the Eye: But I am first now.

Under the Eye: I was not first.

Under the Nose: But I am first now.

Chin: I just want to stay innocent.

Collarbone: I am innocent.

Under the Arm: But my parents are not.

Head: It is not my business.

Eyebrow: I acknowledge my father's first wife (or my mother's first husband).

Side of the Eye: I acknowledge my older half-siblings.

Under the Eye: I accept the order that is.

Intuited Tapping
Tap at least three rounds following your intuited stream of consciousness as it relates to seeing and including the previous family.

Close the Exercise
Choose one of the following to close the exercise.

- Bow your head with a thank you to all seen and unseen.

- Bow the head and torso held for several minutes until the feeling of completion arises.

- Place your hands to the heart with a bow of the head.

- Complete a symbolic physical and energetic closing of your own design.

The Healing Picture

This work is effective when:

- You feel a sense of place.
- You recognize the other family that came before you.
- You see the love between your parents.

Chapter Nine: Children and Loss

*The world may never notice
If a rosebud doesn't bloom
Or even pause to wonder
if the petals fall too soon.*

*But every life that ever forms,
Or ever comes to be
Touches the world in some small way
For all eternity.*

*The little ones we longed for
Were swiftly here and gone.
But the love that was then planted
Is a light that still shines on.*

*And though our arms are empty,
Our hearts know what to do
Every beating of my heart says
I remember you.*

Author unknown[18]

---

[18] This poem is published online under two titles: I Remember You and Little Snowdrop. No copyright information available at this time. If you are the author or have information on copyright, please contact me. It is a beautiful piece of work.

Chapter Nine

Children's Order

The feeling of relief when children are in proper order is quite tangible and clear. By order, I mean acknowledging all children of a parent, whether alive or deceased. If a miscarriage, adoption, or abortion has occurred, we need to recalibrate how we define the order of our children.

My view is that all pregnancies count towards the order of the children. Some constellation facilitators view miscarriages in the first trimester as not counting towards the number of children, but in every client situation I have had, each pregnancy counts and affects the place of the child.

When to Use
This exercise can be helpful when:

- You have had multiple pregnancies.
- There is a pattern of lost pregnancies in the family.
- You know or suspect that your grandmother lost a child.
- You have not felt settled in your place in the family.
- There is a theme of family loss that you cannot escape and you do not understand why.

Setting the Stage
Imagine the mother and father looking at all their children lined up in order from oldest to youngest. Imagine the line-up with only the living children. In the example illustration that follows, the family had three pregnancies but only two children lived. The mother might imagine that she is the mother of two; however, the youngest might feel some sense of being out

Children and Loss

of order because he intrinsically knows he was third but is told he is second.

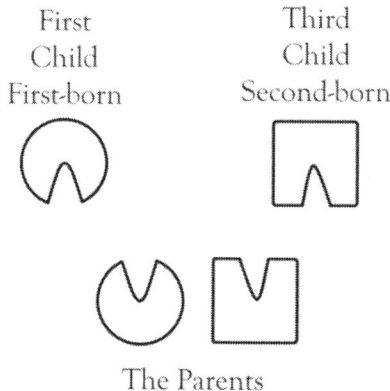

Illustration 20: Parents and Three Children with the Middle Child Unacknowledged

Now sense the line-up with all your children including any who died or were lost during pregnancy or any other way.

Chapter Nine

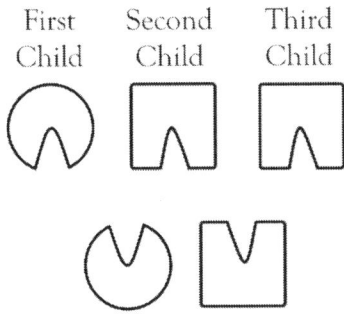

The Parents

Illustration 21: The relief comes from seeing all the children in their right order.

Sensing the Field

Notice the difference in how you feel with the two configurations. Now, look at each of your children one at a time and notice:

- How does it feel to see her in the proper place?
- Do you feel connection?
- Do you feel grief?
- Do you feel love?
- Do you feel hope?

Reiterative Tapping

While tapping the karate chop points, say:

Even though one of my children was missing, I see them all now.

Even though one of my children was missing, I see them all now.

Even though one of my children was missing, I see them all now.

Do one round per expression for two rounds total.

1. You are all my children.
2. You all have a place in my heart.

Cascading Tapping
Tapping on the karate chop points, say:

Even though one of my children was missing, I see them all now.

Even though I did not want to see the lost child, I see them all now.

Even though the pain of seeing the lost child felt too much, in fact not seeing the child was too much.

Moving through the points:

Eyebrow: You are my children.

Side of the Eye: You have all have a place in my heart.

Under the Eye: (to the first child) You are my first.

Under the Nose: (to the second) You are my second.

Chin: (to the third if there is a third) You are the third.

Collarbone: You always are in my heart.

Under the Arm: I am the mother of (#[19]) children.

Head: We are the mother and father of (#) children.

---

[19] # = the total number of pregnancies had.

Intuited Tapping

Do several rounds of tapping following your stream of consciousness based on what you have read so far and the idea of seeing all your children with love.

Close the Exercise

Choose one of the following to close the exercise.

- Bow your head with a thank you to all seen and unseen.

- Bow the head and torso held for several minutes until the feeling of completion arises.

- Place your hands to the heart with a bow of the head.

- Complete a symbolic physical and energetic closing of your own design.

The Healing Picture

This exercise is working when:

- You notice a sense of relief in acknowledging all the children you have.

If you do not feel relief yet, examine your conception history for another pregnancy or a missing twin not yet acknowledged.

Missing Twin

The concept of a twin that was absorbed in utero is called the vanishing twin syndrome. First identified in 1945, experts vary in their estimates of how frequently vanishing twins happen.[20] While it is hard to know if you have a vanishing twin many years later, I have had clients who felt substantially better and more at peace after exploring the idea of a missing twin.

When to Use
- You feel like part of you is missing and you do not understand why.
- You feel out of place with your siblings and no other obvious missing siblings are known.
- You feel like you are depressed or being held back and you have tried many other healing methods.

Setting the Stage
In a standing position, with your body centered, your legs slightly bent, close your eyes and take a deep breath. Tune into your core and acknowledge your life as the child of your mother and father, saying to yourself (out loud or quietly), "I am complete as the child of my mother and father."

Sensing the Field
- Do you feel complete with that statement?
- Do you feel like something or someone is missing?

If you feel a gap, consider the idea of a missing twin.

---

[20] http://www.americanpregnancy.org/multiples/vanishingtwin.html, Sept. 2012.

Chapter Nine

*Illustration 22:
Facing Your Twin*

Imagine a twin standing directly in front of you. You do not have to imagine specific details unless that helps you. You just tune into the energy of a potential twin. How does that feel to you now? If you feel relief, the essential characteristic of progress in this work, then move on to the tapping below. If the tension stays the same, move on to another tapping script.

Reiterative Tapping
While tapping the karate chop points, say:

Even though I did not even know you were missing, part of me knew.

Even though I did not even know you were missing, part of me knew.

Even though I did not even know you were missing, part of me knew.

Moving through the points with the following phrases for a total of three rounds.

1. We did not have enough for both of us to live.
2. I knew "something" was missing.
3. I never thought it was a "somebody".

Back to the set-up points:

Even though we did not have enough for both of us, I honor both of our lives.

Even though we did not have enough for both of us, I honor both of our lives.

Even though we did not have enough for both of us, I honor both of our lives.

Finish with four more rounds:

1. We did not have enough for both of us.
2. I wish we had had enough for both of us.
3. You will always be in my heart.
4. I live my life in honor of both of us.

Cascading Tapping

Tapping on the karate chop points, say:

Even though I did not even know you were missing, part of me knew.

Even though I felt so incomplete, I am open to the idea of feeling complete now.

Even though we did not have enough for both of us, I honor both of our lives.

Moving through the points:

Eyebrow: We did not have enough for both of us.

Side of the Eye: I knew "something" was missing.

Under the Eye: I never thought it was a "somebody".

Under the Nose: Part of me believes it was my fault.

Chin: I am the reason you do not exist.

Collarbone: I am the reason you did not survive.

Under the Arm: I lived; you did not.

Head: I lived; you did not.

Eyebrow: We did not have enough for both of us.

Side of the Eye: I have missed you.

Under the Eye: I have missed you.

Under the Nose: Even though you did not survive, I hold you close in my heart.

Chin: I wish we had enough for both of us.

Collarbone: I am the only one who knows you.

Under the Arm: You will always be in my heart.

Head: I live my life in honor of both of us.

Intuited Tapping
Tap at least three rounds following your intuited stream of consciousness as it relates to how you feel about the idea of reconnecting with your in-utero twin.

Close the Exercise
Choose one of the following to close the exercise.

- Bow your head with a thank you to all seen and unseen.

- Bow the head and torso held for several minutes until the feeling of completion arises.

- Place your hands to the heart with a bow of the head.

- Complete a symbolic physical and energetic closing of your own design.

The Healing Picture

The healing picture includes:

- As you imagine yourself as a twin, you feel invigorated and full of life.

- You are ready to move forward with your life.

- You can imagine your twin next to you when you need to or want to.

- You feel complete as yourself while recognizing that you once were half of a pair.

- You are ready to engage with your life.

Chapter Nine

Miscarriage

Those of us who have experienced the loss of a child have grieved; however, I still find that miscarriages are not healed fully. The missing piece of this healing is often the father not being included fully in the grieving and both parents claiming their love for the unborn child.

When to Use
- You have experienced a miscarriage.
- Your parents experienced a miscarriage.
- There is a theme of loss in the family and you suspect miscarriages further back in the family line.

Setting the Stage
This exercise is written from the perspective that you are the mother. You can use it for a third party by considering yourself as a surrogate and doing surrogate tapping.

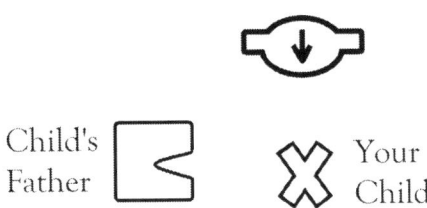

Illustration 23: You and the Father Seeing the Child

Imagine your child lying on the ground in front of you.[21] Do not imagine a specific age; sense the entire gestalt being of the person. Imagine your partner, the other parent of the child, standing next to you while you look at this child you lost.

Sensing the Field
- Are you able to imagine looking at your child?
- Do you look away instead?
- Do you feel grief?
- Do you feel numb?
- Do you feel love?
- Is your partner looking as well?
- Can you recognize this loss as a loss for both of you?

Reiterative Tapping
While tapping the karate chop points, say:

Even though we lost you, you are still in our hearts.

Even though we lost you, you are still in our hearts.

Even though we lost you, you are still in our hearts.

Do one round for each expression for a total of three rounds.

1. This loss of our child.

---

[21] This position on the floor represents the death of that person. We will use this format with any early death.

Chapter Nine

2. We both lost you.

3. You always have a place in our hearts.

Cascading Tapping

Tapping on the karate chop points, say:

Even though we did not get to know you, you are still our child.

Even though we lost you, you are still in our hearts.

Even though we are still grieving your loss to us, we see the love that is here.

Eyebrow: We were excited to know you were coming.

Side of the Eye: We were excited to meet you.

Under the Eye: And then we lost you.

Under the Nose: We lost you too soon.

Chin: I as the mother grieve you.

Collarbone: I as the father grieve you.

Under the Arm: We both grieve you.

Head: We were making room for you in our hearts when you died.

Eyebrow: That room still exists, empty and abandoned.

Side of the Eye: It felt like a hole.

Under the Eye: And now we feel the love we still have for you.

Under the Nose: You do have a place in our hearts.

Chin: You are in our hearts.

Collarbone: This loss of our child.

Under the Arm: We see you.

Head: We love and see you as one of our children.

Intuited Tapping
Tap at least three rounds following your intuited stream of consciousness as it relates to seeing and including this unborn child.

Close the Exercise
Choose one of the following to close the exercise.

- Bow your head with a thank you to all seen and unseen.

- Bow the head and torso held for several minutes until the feeling of completion arises.

- Place your hands to the heart with a bow of the head.

- Complete a symbolic physical and energetic closing of your own design.

The Healing Picture
This exercise is working when:

- You feel your child as included in your family.

- You have felt and released the grief.

- You realize that both you and the other parent need to see and acknowledge this child.

After you complete this exercise, you may want to revisit or visit the Children's Order exercise found on page 122.

Chapter Nine

Adoption

Biological Parents and the Child

Being able to see the bonds as well the losses in adoptive situations can bring a sense of ease to all the family members. The biological parents are the focus of this first set of tapping scripts.

When to Use
- There is an adoption in the immediate family.
- There is an adoption in the ancestral family.

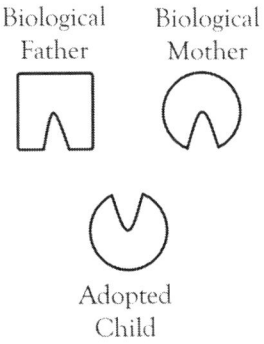

Illustration 24: The Biological Parents and Their Child

Setting the Stage
Imagine the biological parents facing their biological child. You do not have to imagine the child at any particular age;

instead think of the total energy of the child at all ages. The length of time since the adoption does not matter.

Sensing the Field
Tune into the bond between the biological parents and child. Notice both the sense of loss and the love that is still living.

Reiterative Tapping
While tapping the karate chop points, say:

Even though we gave you away, and the price we paid was dear, we are willing to see the love we have for you.

Tap one round per expression for two rounds.

1. We gave you life.

2. We gave you life and then we gave you away.

Back to the set-up points:

Even though we gave you life, and the rest you got from others, we are open to accepting the decision we made.

Tap one round per expression for two more rounds.

1. The rest you got from others.

2. You are always in our hearts.

Cascading Tapping
Tapping on the karate chop points, say:

Even though we gave you away, and the feelings are unbearable, we are willing to see our loss.

Even though we gave you away, and while it was the best decision we could make at the time, we acknowledge what it cost you and what it cost us.

Chapter Nine

Even though we gave you away, and the price we paid was dear, we are willing to see the love we have for you.

Even though we gave you life, and the rest you got from others, we are open to accepting the decision we made.

Eyebrow: We gave you life.

Side of the Eye: And then we gave you away.

Under the Eye: The loss was ours.

Under the Nose: The loss was yours.

Chin: We gave you life.

Collarbone: The rest you got from others.

Under the Arm: You will always be in our hearts.

Head: You always are in our hearts.

Eyebrow: You always were in our hearts.

Side of the Eye: Our hearts are open to you.

Under the Eye: We are willing to feel the pain of giving you away.

Under the Nose: We are willing to feel our love for you.

Chin: We acknowledge the love we have for each other.

Collarbone: We acknowledge what it cost you.

Under the Arm: We acknowledge what it cost us.

Head: We acknowledge the gift of your life.

Intuited Tapping
Tap at least three rounds following your intuited stream of consciousness, acknowledging both the loss and the love.

Close the Exercise
Choose one of the following to close the exercise.

- Bow your head with a thank you to all seen and unseen.

- Bow the head and torso held for several minutes until the feeling of completion arises.

- Place your hands to the heart with a bow of the head.

- Complete a symbolic physical and energetic closing of your own design.

The Healing Picture
This tapping is done when:

- You feel the love you have for the child.

- You feel the connection you have with the child.

- You can acknowledge the price paid by all.

Adoptive Parents and the Biological Parents

Whether the parents have met each other or not in real life, this tapping script addresses some of the areas parents need to address at the family matrix level.

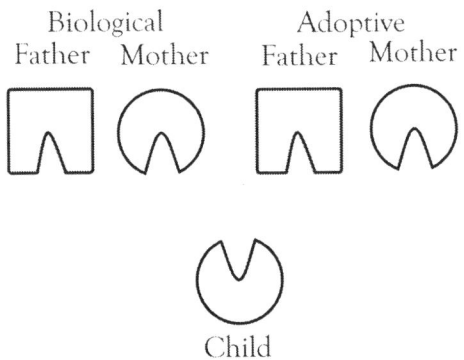

Illustration 25: Child Facing Both Sets of Parents

Setting the Stage
Imagine the two sets of parents facing the child. Whether the biological parents are still together or not, have them stand side by side.

Sensing the Field
- What do you notice between the two sets of parents?
- Are they able to look at each other?
- Do they acknowledge each other?
- Do they see their connection and love for the child?

Reiterative Tapping from the Biological Parents
While tapping the karate chop points, say:

Even though we mourn the loss of our child, we thank you for taking care of her.

Even though we mourn the loss of our child, we thank you for taking care of her.

Even though we mourn the loss of our child, we thank you for taking care of her.

Tap one round per expression for a total of four rounds.

1. We miss her.
2. We thank you.
3. We gave her life.
4. You gave her the rest.

Cascading Tapping
Tapping on the karate chop points, say:

Even though we mourn the loss of our child, we thank you for taking care of her.

Even though it was our choice to lose our child, we claim our place as her biological parents.

Even though our loss was your gain, we acknowledge the price you paid for taking care of her.

Even though we gave her life, you gave her the rest.

Eyebrow: Thank you for taking care of her.

Side of the Eye: Thank you for loving her.

Under the Eye: We gave her life.

Under the Nose: You gave her the rest.

Chin: We gave her life.

Collarbone: You gave her the rest.

Under the Arm: We honor our intertwined paths.

Head: We honor your commitment and love.

Intuited Tapping
Tap at least three rounds following your intuited stream of consciousness as it relates to what you have read above.

Close the Exercise
Choose one of the following to close the exercise.

- Bow your head with a thank you to all seen and unseen.
- Bow the head and torso held for several minutes until the feeling of completion arises.
- Place your hands to the heart with a bow of the head.
- Complete a symbolic physical and energetic closing of your own design.

The Healing Picture
This tapping is complete when:

- You feel appreciation for the adoptive parents.

Reiterative Tapping from Adoptive Parents
While tapping the karate chop points, say:

Even though you gave him life and we gave him a life, we are open to seeing the love between all of us.

Even though you gave him life and we gave him a life, we are open to seeing the love between all of us.

Even though you gave him life and we gave him a life, we are open to seeing the love between all of us.

One round per expression for two rounds.

1. Thank you for giving him life.
2. We acknowledge all that it cost you and all that it cost him.

Cascading Tapping

Tapping on the karate chop points, say:

Even though you gave him up, and part of us cannot understand that, we are open to seeing the love that exists.

Even though we sometimes feel like do not have the same bond you do, we acknowledge both your bond and ours.

Even though we did not give her life, we did give her a life and we acknowledge what it cost you and what it cost her.

Moving through the points:

Eyebrow: You gave her up.

Side of the Eye: We chose her out of love.

Under the Eye: You gave her up.

Under the Nose: We chose her.

Chin: She needed both you and us.

Collarbone: We are open to seeing what it cost you.

Under the Arm: We are open to seeing what it cost us.

Head: We are open to seeing what it cost her.

Intuited Tapping
Tap at least three rounds following your intuition and feelings as you address and accept the biological parents and their role in your child's life.

Close the Exercise
Choose one of the following to close the exercise.

- Bow your head with a thank you to all seen and unseen.

- Bow the head and torso held for several minutes until the feeling of completion arises.

- Place your hands to the heart with a bow of the head.

- Complete a symbolic physical and energetic closing of your own design.

The Healing Picture
This exercise is completed when:

- You feel appreciation for the biological parents.

- You see both of your places in your child's life.

Terminated Pregnancies

> *"There was a place in my heart beginning to be made for that child, a little indentation I don't think will ever be filled."*
>
> Michael Chabon[22]

If you have terminated a pregnancy and are now facing any limitations or issues with your career, your current children, or relationships, consider these tapping exercises that follow. Abortion can be a challenging situation for any subsequent children, not to mention the stress it places on the parents. Four views are considered when we work with terminated pregnancies: the mother, the father, the lost child, and any subsequent children. I have included scripts for the first three.

When to Use
- You have terminated a pregnancy.
- You face issues with your career, current children, or relationships.
- You know of abortions with your mother, grandmother, or other family members.

---

[22] Belinda Luscombe, "10 Questions: Pulitzer Price-winning novelist Michael Chabon on race, fatherhood, and writing box-office flops," Time, October 1, 2012, p.64.

Chapter Nine

The Mother's Perspective

Setting the Stage

As the mother, imagine the energy of your unborn child facing you. Do not picture a specific age or look, just the timeless gestalt energy of the child who was conceived by you and another.

Illustration 26: Facing Your Unborn Child

Sensing the Field

- What do you notice in your body?
- What do you notice in your heart?
- What thoughts are you thinking?
- Do you feel detached?
- Do you feel love?

Notice how turning away produces constriction and looking toward produces relief.

Reiterative Tapping

While tapping on the karate chop points, say:

Even though the time was not right for this child, and I have wanted to put the events and feelings behind me, I am willing to open my heart to this child.

Even though the time was not right for this child, and I have wanted to put all the events and feelings behind me, I am willing to open my heart to this child.

Even though the time was not right for this child, and I have wanted to put the feelings and events behind me, I am willing to open my heart to this child.

Moving through the points, tap one round on each of the following statements for a total of four rounds.

1. The time was not right.
2. I did not want this child.
3. I chose not to have this child.
4. We chose not to have this child.

Cascading Tapping

Tapping on the karate chop points, say:

Even though the time was not right for this child, and I have wanted to put the feelings and events all behind me, I am willing to open my heart to this child.

Even though the time was not right, and part of me did not want this child, I acknowledge the part of me that did want this child.

Even though I did want this child, and the time was not right, I take responsibility for my actions and open my heart to this child.

Tap on the points as indicated.

Eyebrow: The time was not right; I did not want this child.

Side of the Eye: I did not want this child.

Under the Eye: We did not want this child.

Under the Nose: We chose not to have this child.

Chin: I chose not to have this child.

Collarbone: He chose not to have this child.

Under the Arm: We chose not to.

Head: Part of me wanted this child.

Eyebrow: All of me wanted this child.

Side of the Eye: The time was not right.

Under the Eye: The time was not right.

Under the Nose: This child has a place in my heart.

Chin: I see you.

Collarbone: I acknowledge you.

Under the Arm: You will always have a place in my heart.

Head: You are my child.

Intuited Tapping

After reading the preceding scripts for ideas, tap at least three rounds following your intuited stream of consciousness and feelings.

Close the Exercise

Choose one of the following to close the exercise.

- Bow your head with a thank you to all seen and unseen.

- Bow the head and torso held for several minutes until the feeling of completion arises.

- Place your hands to the heart with a bow of the head.

- Complete a symbolic physical and energetic closing of your own design.

The Healing Picture
This exercise has done its work when:

- You think of your child who did not live and can feel a connection.

- You feel him or her in your heart.

- You know they just want to be seen by you and loved.

- You acknowledge the connection.

Chapter Nine

From the Mother to the Father

The father's role in the abortion also needs to be addressed. Often a hidden, or not-so-hidden, blame is poisoning the healing. If this is the case, the following script can help.

Reiterative Tapping
While tapping the karate chop points, say:

Even though I blame you for this decision, I am open to the idea of accepting my part in it all.

Even though I blame you for this decision, I am open to the idea of accepting my part in it all.

Even though I blame you for this decision, I am open to the idea of accepting my part in it all.

Moving through the points, do one round on each of the following statements for a total of four rounds.

1. I blame you, I blame us, and I blame myself.
2. I have shut off my heart because of what we did.
3. We created life together.
4. And we ended it together.

Cascading Tapping
Tapping on the karate chop points, say:

Even though I blame you for this decision, I am open to the idea of accepting my part.

Even though I needed you for this baby, and you were not available, I am open to the idea of accepting my part.

Even though this decision drove us apart, I am open to seeing the love we had together and taking responsibility for my part.

Tapping on the points, say the following:

Eyebrow: I blame you.

Side of the Eye: I blame myself.

Under the Eye: I blame both of us.

Under the Nose: I needed you for this child.

Chin: I needed you for this child.

Collarbone: And you were not available.

Under the Arm: I was not available.

Head: I have shut off my heart because of what happened.

Eyebrow: I have shut off my soul because of what we did.

Side of the Eye: We created life.

Under the Eye: And we ended it.

Under the Nose: We created life.

Chin: And we ended it.

Collarbone: I take responsibility for what we did.

Under the Arm: I take responsibility for what I did.

Head: We did it together.

Intuited Tapping

Tap at least three rounds following your intuited stream of consciousness as it relates to your feelings about the other parent's role in the abortion decision. Ultimately you both take responsibility for your parts.

Close the Exercise
Choose one of the following to close the exercise.

- Bow your head with a thank you to all seen and unseen.

- Bow the head and torso held for several minutes until the feeling of completion arises.

- Place your hands to the heart with a bow of the head.

- Complete a symbolic physical and energetic closing of your own design.

The Healing Picture
This exercise is done when:

- You can face your decision and your partner and take responsibility without feeling shame, anger, or grief.

- You face your unborn child without collapsing emotionally or energetically.

Mother to Child

Imagine facing the unborn child but this time you will speak as if speaking directly to him or her. Do this round of tapping only after you have done the tapping for the mother and father.

Illustration 27: Facing the Child Together

Reiterative Tapping
While tapping the karate chop points, say:

Even though it hurt too much to remember you, we remember you now.

Even though it hurt too much to remember you, we remember you now.

Even though it hurt too much to remember you, we remember you now.

Moving through the points, do one round on each of the following statements for a total of three rounds.

1. You will always have a place in our hearts.

2. We do remember you.

3. We remember you even as we move forward with other children.

Cascading Tapping

Tapping on the karate chop points, say:

Even though we gave you up, you will always have a place in our hearts.

Even though you were our first, and we were denying you your place, we claim you now as our first.[23]

Even though it hurt too much to remember you, we remember you now.

Moving through the points:

Eyebrow: We chose not to have you.

Side of the Eye: You will always have a place in our hearts.

Under the Eye: We chose not to have you.

Under the Nose: And we do remember you.

Chin: We chose not to have you.

Collarbone: And we remember you as we move forward with other children.

Under the Arm: We remember you.

Head: You have a place in our hearts.

---

[23] Change the word "first" as needed to reflect whatever appropriate place the child was in the order of pregnancies.

Intuited Tapping

Tap at least three rounds following your intuited stream of consciousness as you tell your child you remember her/him and she/he will always be in your heart.

Close the Exercise

Choose one of the following to close the exercise.

- Bow your head with a thank you to all seen and unseen.

- Bow the head and torso held for several minutes until the feeling of completion arises.

- Place your hands to the heart with a bow of the head.

- Complete a symbolic physical and energetic closing of your own design.

The Healing Picture

This portion of the exercise is complete when you look at your child and smile.

Chapter Nine

No Children

I have worked with several clients who had lost their parents and were crippled by the grief. We did lots of EFT on the loss of the parents, but I found one key piece was blocking the healing. These clients had no children and while they felt a strong connection to their deceased parents, they needed something forward-facing to call the love from them. No love was flowing forward from the clients and so they were connected to the past in ways that did not serve them. Whatever the reasons are for not having children, if you can claim the creative expression that is in your life, you can feel the magnetism of life and of giving birth to something.

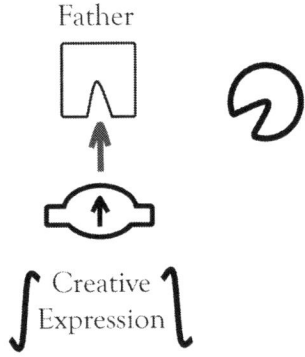

Illustration 28: Connection to Deceased Father with Lost Connection to Creative Expression

When to Use
- When you do not have any living children.
- You feel a lack of creative expression.
- If you lost a child in pregnancy or birth, do the miscarriage piece first.

Setting the Stage
Imagine in front of you an energy representing your creative expression in this life: your work, your art, your passion, or your energy. You can imagine your parents standing behind you if you desire.

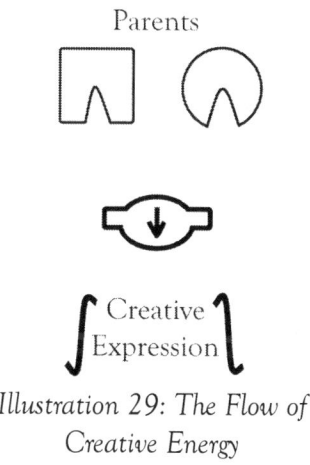

Illustration 29: The Flow of Creative Energy

Sensing the Field
- How do you feel about this creative expression?
- Do you feel a sadness?
- Do you notice judgment?
- Are you aware of a numbness?

- Do you feel a sense of loss?
- Do you notice excitement?
- Do you feel joy?
- Do you sense delight?
- Do you feel anticipation?

Reiterative Tapping

While tapping on the set-up points, say:

Even though I do not have children, and all the love flowing through the generations has stopped with me, I am open to accepting myself.

Even though I do not have children, and all the love flowing through the generations has stopped with me, I am open to accepting myself.

Even though I do not have children, and all the love flowing through the generations has stopped with me, I am open to accepting myself.

Tap on the points, doing one round per expression for a total of five rounds.

1. I do not have children.
2. The love has stopped with me.
3. My ancestors' lives have stopped with me.
4. I am open to seeing my creative expression as love.
5. I am open to seeing the love and energy flow from my ancestors through me and out to the world.

Cascading Tapping

Tapping on the karate chop points, say:

Even though I do not have children, and all my ancestors' creation has gone to waste, I am open to accepting myself.

Even though I do not have children, and all the love flowing through the generations has stopped with me, I am open to accepting myself.

Even though I do not have children, and all the pain flowing through the generations has stopped with me, I am open to accepting myself and my expression of love in the world.

Moving through the points:

Eyebrow: I do not have children.

Side of the Eye: The love stopped with me.

Under the Eye: The flow stopped with me.

Under the Nose: I have no life purpose without children.

Chin: This loss of life and creative expression.

Collarbone: I do not have children.

Under the Arm: The love stopped with me.

Head: I do not have children.

Moving to the affirmative:

Eyebrow: I am open to seeing my work as love.

Side of the Eye: I am open to seeing my creative expression as love.

Under the Eye: I am open to giving back through my presence.

Under the Nose: I am open to loving the world.

Chin: I am open to the creative expressions of my life.

Collarbone: I am a creative force.

Under the Arm: I am open to seeing the love and energy in my life.

Head: The love from my ancestors flows through me and to the world.

Intuited Tapping
Tap at least three rounds following your intuited stream of consciousness as it relates to your expressing love in the world. You are not trying to replace having children, you are just keeping the flow of love going.

Close the Exercise
- Bow your head with a thank you to all seen and unseen.

- Bow the head and torso held for several minutes until the feeling of completion arises.

- Place your hands to the heart with a bow of the head.

- Complete a symbolic physical and energetic closing of your own design.

The Healing Picture
This exercise has worked when:

- You feel the love and support flowing from your great-grandparents, through your grandparents to your parents to you and then out forward beyond you.

Chapter Ten: Fate, Connection, and Appreciation

Feeling Stuck and Not Understanding

When to Use
- You feel stuck or feel resistance thinking about your family system.
- You feel heavy or thick thinking about your family system.
- You do not know what happened specifically in your family.

Setting the Stage
Knowing that family information and energy is available for you to access and that you are one component of a system much bigger than you can be a relief for those of us who have done our work but still feel the heaviness of the larger system. Sometimes, however, we do not understand the heaviness or know where to begin. This script might open up that feeling of heaviness and show you where to look next for your reconnection with the matrix.

Sensing the Field
Take a deep breath, relax your body, and think of your family field extending backwards in time. Feel your body. Notice the tension and the heaviness that arises. You might also notice relief as you take the focus off of yourself and on to the larger system.

Chapter Ten

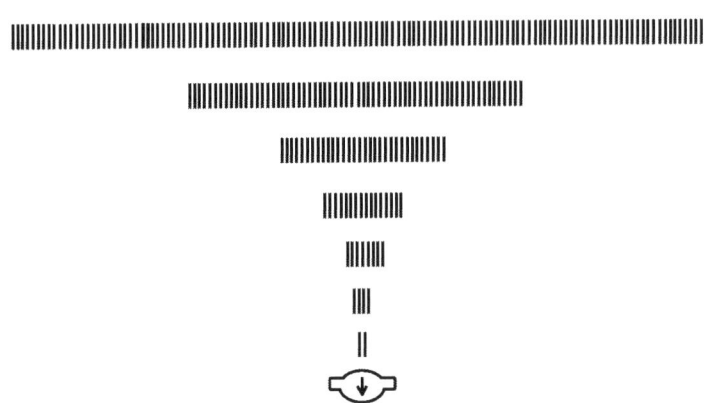

Illustration 30: Many Generations Behind You

Reiterative Tapping

While tapping on the karate chop points, say:

Even though I feel stuck, tense, and frustrated, I am open to the idea of seeing the larger picture.

Even though I feel stuck, tense, and frustrated, I am open to the idea of seeing the larger picture.

Even though I feel stuck, tense, and frustrated, I am open to the idea of seeing the larger picture.

Do one round per expression for a total of four rounds.

1. This feels heavy.
2. I wonder where the heaviness comes from.
3. I wonder where the flow of love and life is disrupted.
4. I am open to seeing the love that is possible.

Cascading Tapping

Tapping on the karate chop points, say:

Even though I feel stuck and tense and I know I am missing something, I am open to seeing what is next.

Even though I feel stuck, tense, and frustrated, I am open to the idea of seeing the larger picture.

Even though I feel tense and disconnected, I am open to the idea of seeing the love that is possible.

Moving through the points:

Eyebrow: This feels so heavy.

Side of the Eye: I do not know where to start.

Under the Eye: I do not know if I can "fix" this heaviness.

Under the Nose: I do not know if I can stand to feel the pain that is here.

Chin: It is not my responsibility.

Collarbone: And I can feel the heaviness.

Under the Arm: I feel too much here to consider.

Head: I do not know where to begin untangling the flow.

Eyebrow: I am open to the idea that I can start anyplace.

Side of the Eye: I am open to the idea that I can start several generations ago where it is safer for me.

Under the Eye: I am open to the idea that I can observe my family system at a distance.

Under the Nose: I am open to the idea that I am not responsible for all the pain I see.

Chin: I am open to the idea that each and every family member is capable of living their fate honorably.

Collarbone: I am open to the idea that some of my family wants me to live life joyfully.

Under the Arm: I am open to the idea that the rest of my family needs to be seen.

Head: I am open to the idea of seeing and also being at peace with my life.

Intuited Tapping
Tap at least three rounds following your intuited stream of consciousness as it relates to what you have read.

Close the Exercise
Choose one of the following to close the exercise.

- Bow your head with a thank you to all seen and unseen.

- Bow the head and torso held for several minutes until the feeling of completion arises.

- Place your hands to the heart with a bow of the head.

- Complete a symbolic physical and energetic closing of your own design.

The Healing Picture
This exercise has done its work when:

- You start to feel a glimmer of energy, excitement, or possibility.

- You get an idea of who or what needs to be seen.

Chapter Ten

Uncomfortable Secrets

Fate is a term used in formal Family Constellations and I find it is a powerful word indeed. It refers to the unique path of each of our lives. When we see and honor the fate of another, we see their unique path and we see the strength and honor in how they lived. It does not imply being a victim but does include seeing the various losses and pain involved. My fate is to be born into my family. Your fate is to be born into yours. It just is.

In 2012 a show was on television called "Who Do You Think You Are?" On the show, current celebrities dug into their past and found out more about their ancestors and where they came from. (I notice that more and more mainstream resources and media are focusing on ancestral insights which I find indicative of a desired ancestral healing and connection.) In the show, Reba McEntire, an American performing artist, was one of the participants and found out several facts about her family that were disturbing. [24]

This show points to some interesting consequences when we research our past. We might expect to find out great things about our families, and we might. But at the same time, family myths get de-bunked and family secrets get uncovered. It is easy to judge past behavior by today's standards. We might ask questions like:

- How could this person marry so many times?

---

[24] The show aired originally March 2, 2012 on NBC. She discovered that one of her ancestors was a slave owner and that another had been an indentured servant.

- How did that person keep this secret?
- How did this person own slaves?
- How did that person leave?
- How did this person stay?

Robin Grille writes of the evolution of families and child-rearing practices in *Parenting for a Peaceful World*. Reading his book, I am struck by the changes in our cultures over time and realize that we truly cannot judge the actions of others in the past by our standards today. We instead can recognize the evolution and celebrate both the past and the evolution.

While researching our past can satisfy a curiosity, its true purpose is to make us more connected to who we are. We are who we are because of our past, not in spite of. Unearthing secrets does not change who we are and can bring us a dignity in living our lives as we accept our genetic lineage.

When to Use
You have been digging into your family's past and already know some disturbing news about your family history.

Setting the Stage
Think about your family past and any new information you have uncovered that feels challenging.

Sensing the Field
As you think about this family past, take a deep breath. Be open to what you are feeling for yourself and be open to the idea of accepting without judging what came before you.

Reiterative Tapping
Tapping on the karate chop points, say:

Chapter Ten

Even though I am disappointed in where I came from, I am open to the idea of accepting myself and my history.

Even though I am disappointed in where I came from, I am open to the idea of accepting myself and my history.

Even though I am disappointed in where I came from, I am open to the idea of accepting myself and my history.

Do one full round for each phrase that follows for a total of five rounds:

1. I am disappointed in what they did.
2. I do not understand it.
3. I am here regardless.
4. I am open to seeing my value and the gift of my being alive.
5. Without them, I would not be alive.

Cascading Tapping

Tapping on the karate chop points, say:

Even though I am disappointed in what I know about my family, I am open to the idea of loving and accepting myself.

Even though I am disappointed in where I came from, I am open to the idea of accepting myself and knowing my value.

Even though I do not understand these past decisions and events, I am open to the idea of accepting my life.

Moving through the points:

Eyebrow: I am disappointed in what I found out.

Side of the Eye: I am disappointed in my past.

Under the Eye: I do not understand why they did what they did.

Under the Nose: I am open to seeing their path as theirs.

Chin: I am open to seeing they did the best they could with what they had.

Under the Arm: Even though I am not open to seeing what they did as good, I am open to the idea of not judging it.

Eyebrow: This family history and this family secret.

Side of the Eye: I am open to seeing their path and their fate.

Under the Eye: My fate was to be born into this family.

Under the Nose: I am open to accepting who I am.

Chin: I am open to accepting the gift of life.

Collarbone: I accept the gift of my life.

Under the Arm: I am open to the life that came to me from my ancestors.

Head: I do not understand and I accept the gift of my life.

Intuited Tapping
Tap at least three rounds following your intuited stream of consciousness as it relates to how you feel about what you have discovered about your family.

Close the Exercise
Choose one of the following to close the exercise.

- Bow your head with a thank you to all seen and unseen.

Chapter Ten

- Bow the head and torso held for several minutes until the feeling of completion arises.

- Place your hands to the heart with a bow of the head.

- Complete a symbolic physical and energetic closing of your own design.

The Healing Picture

The healing has started when:

- No matter the secrets you have discovered, you feel the gift of your life.

- No matter the path of those who came before you, you can feel the delight in your life.

- You realize that your unique life comes from all the ancestors who came before you.

Great-Grandparents Connection

The outcome of looking at different family entanglements is to come to a place where we feel energized and supported by who we are. We come from two parents, four grandparents, eight great-grandparents and sixteen great-great-grandparents. Here is an exercise to strengthen the connection to each quadrant of your lineage. Most people have not met their great-grandparents or did so when they were young. The great-grandparents are often a missing yet strong link to the past.

When to Use

- You have done some of the other scripts and are feeling complete.

- You feel like some work wants to be done but you do not know any specifics.

Setting the Stage

As you know, you come from four sets of great-grandparents parents:

- Your mother's mother's parents, in my case, the Simmons.

- Your mother's father's parents, in my case, the Kimpels.

- Your father's mother's parents, in my case, the Broggers.

- Your father's father's parents, in my case, the Halls.

Having a strong connection to each of these sets of great-grandparents is pivotal to feeling a strong life force.

Sensing the Field

Tune into one set of parents' parents' parents at a time. Take a deep breath; say their family name and sense the connection to these ancestors. Feel it in your body, your heart, and even your mind.

- Do you feel connection?
- Do you feel pride?
- Do you feel love?
- Do you feel sadness?
- Do you feel disconnection?
- Do you feel regrets?
- Do you feel anger?
- Do you feel love?

Choose the appropriate tapping script that follows and do for each set of great-grandparents. For each set of great-grandparents, I recommend making note of three things. What is the initial sense of connection? What is the sense of connection after tapping? What thoughts or feelings changed with tapping?

Fate, Connection, and Appreciation

Mother's   Mother's
Mother's   Mother's
Father   Mother

*Illustration 31: Facing Your
Great-Grandparents on Your
Mother's Mother's Side*

Mother's Mother's Parents'

Surname:

Initial Sense of Connection:

Sense of Connection After Tapping:

What Happened During the Rounds of Tapping:

Chapter Ten

Mother's Father's Father   Mother's Father's Mother

Illustration 32: Facing Your Great-Grandparents on Your Mother's Father's Side

Mother's Father's Parents'

Surname:

Initial Sense of Connection:

Sense of Connection After Tapping:

What Happened During the Rounds of Tapping:

Fate, Connection, and Appreciation

Illustration 33: Facing Your Great-Grandparents on Your Father's Mother's Side

Father's Mother's Parents'

Surname:

Initial Sense of Connection:

Sense of Connection After Tapping:

What Happened During the Rounds of Tapping:

Chapter Ten

Father's Father's Father   Father's Father's Mother

Illustration 34: Your Great-Grandparents on Your Father's Father's Side

Father's Father's Parents'

Surname:

Initial Sense of Connection:

Sense of Connection After Tapping:

What Happened During the Rounds of Tapping:

Reiterative Tapping for Disconnection

While tapping the karate chop points, say:

Even though I feel the disconnection, I am open to seeing with love the fate of my ancestors.

Even though I feel the disconnection, I am open to seeing with love the fate of my ancestors.

Even though I feel the disconnection, I am open to seeing with love the fate of my ancestors.

Do one round of tapping for each expression for a total of six rounds.

1. This heavy heart.
2. This family loss.
3. This mother's loss.
4. This father's loss.
5. The fate of my great-grandparents.
6. I receive the gift of life from them and the rest I leave with them.

Cascading Tapping for Disconnection

Tapping on the karate chop points, say:

Even though I sense heartbreak, I look with respect at the fate of this family, my family.

Even though I sense a great loss, a family separated by war, by an ocean, by another strife, I look with respect at the fate of this family.

Chapter Ten

Even though I feel the disconnection, I am open to seeing with love the fate of my ancestors.

Moving through the points:

Eyebrow: This loss years ago.

Side of the Eye: These heavy hearts.

Under the Eye: This lack of joy.

Under the Nose: This lack of love.

Chin: I wish I knew what happened.

Collarbone: My heart longs to feel the connection again.

Under the Arm: These tears.

Head: I am open to feeling it all.

Eyebrow: Not knowing their story.

Side of the Eye: Not feeling their love.

Under the Eye: Seeing the gift of life they passed on.

Under the Nose: Feeling their duty and path.

Chin: Feeling their choices and sacrifices.

Collarbone: I do not understand.

Under the Arm: I do not know.

Head: I do not understand.

Eyebrow: This mother's loss.

Side of the Eye: This father's loss.

Under the Eye: I can still feel it all the years through.

Under the Nose: I feel the loss in my DNA.

Chin: I am open to the idea of respecting their path.

Collarbone: I see their path, the path of Mr. and Mrs. [insert name here].

Under the Arm: I take my place as their great-grandchild.

Head: I accept the gift of my life.

Intuited Tapping for Disconnection
Tap several rounds following your intuited stream of consciousness as it relates to your great-grandparents, your desire to connect, and the acknowledgment of the feeling of disconnection.

Reiterative Tapping for Connection
Tapping on the karate chop points, say:

As I joyfully name my place as their great-grandchild, I feel my heart and body fill with love generations strong.

As I joyfully name my place as their great-grandchild, I feel my heart and body fill with love generations strong.

As I joyfully name my place as their great-grandchild, I feel my heart and body fill with love generations strong.

Tap one round for each expression for a total of three rounds.

1. This family pride.
2. This family legacy.
3. I am proud to be the great-grandchild of the [insert family name here.]

Chapter Ten

Cascading Tapping for Connection
Tapping on the karate chop points, say:

As I tune into my great-grandparents, I feel love and appreciation.

As I tune into their presence, I feel powerful and energized.

As I joyfully name my place as their great-grandchild, I feel my heart and body fill with love generations strong.

Moving through the points:

Eyebrow: This family legacy.

Side of the Eye: This family pride.

Under the Eye: I am proud to be the great-grandchild of the [insert family name here].

Under the Nose: Even though I did not know them, I feel the love from them.

Chin: My heart glows and expands.

Collarbone: They are available to me.

Under the Arm: I live my unique life knowing I have their love and blessings.

Head: I can feel the connection.

Eyebrow: I can feel their pride.

Side of the Eye: I can feel their love.

Under the Eye: I live in honor of my ancestors.

Under the Nose: I live with their love and blessings.

Chin: I live my life fully, showing honor to them.

Collarbone: I live fully expressed.

Under the Arm: I live fully loved.

Head: I live fully supported.

Intuited Tapping for Connection
Tap several rounds following your intuited stream of consciousness as it relates to your connection to this set of ancestors and the feelings of connection and love.

Close the Exercise
Choose one of the following to close the exercise.

- Bow your head with a thank you to all seen and unseen.

- Bow the head and torso held for several minutes until the feeling of completion arises.

- Place your hands to the heart with a bow of the head.

- Complete a symbolic physical and energetic closing of your own design.

The Healing Picture
This tapping is working when:

- You feel the love and support and pure delight in who you are.

- You feel energized from the flow of love from your great-grandparents.

- You can access this feeling any time you desire.

***

Afterword

What Is Possible

Imagine love flowing from one generation to the next, from older to younger, generation to generation. Imagine that love rooted in one's homeland, reaching forward through the generations, feeding, nourishing, and expanding. Imagine the love flowing from parent to child, parent to child.

Imagine that love so strong and connected that every person lost is included, every bump smoothed. Imagine strong rivers of connection flowing strongly and vibrantly. Everyone touched by that river knows they matter, they have a place, they are making a difference.

Imagine each generation so connected and rooted that they are a boundless resource of love and respect for the next generation.

This is what is possible for each of us.

With Appreciation

I have been fortunate to have supportive, smart, and innovative people in my life. My love and appreciation go to:

My Family

My grandparents and their respective ancestors and homelands of Norway, Germany, England, and where ever came before Newfoundland.

My parents, who gave me life. My mother in particular who taught me to be brave, strong, unique and even a tad bit quirky. And my father who taught me to be loyal, loving, and successful.

My brother, whose journey has touched me deeply.

My husband, Jim, who supports, grounds, questions and encourages me.

My children who make my heart shine. My unborn first child, you truly have a place in our hearts. My son and firstborn, Matthew, who both challenges me and cheers me along the way. Samantha, my firstborn daughter, who was by my side at many a coffee shop as I did my writing and gave me her artistic input on layout and design. And my youngest, Amanda, who takes a keen interest in my website and wants to run my shop.

My Colleagues and Friends

Julie Aha, who journeyed with me through several years of growth and shows me the graciousness and wisdom of the body.

Sunday Cote, a fellow spiritual journeyer with a gentle grounded wise way and unwavering friendship.

Yael, my incredibly committed web designer, editor, and kindred spiritual journeyer, who understands this work at a profoundly deep level.

My fellow mothers whose insights, compassion, and commitment inspire and ground me: Teresa Brett, Kathy Brown, Josha Grant, Linda Friedman Jones, Pia Mark, Karen McLaughlin, and Marian Mills.

Paul Zelizer and Sejual Shah, innovative business and spiritual coaches, co-creators of Business Energetics, who have been energetic supporters of Family Energetics for many years. They gently challenged and invited me to step into my power and share this work more broadly.

My Teachers

Jessica Dibbs, leader of the Inspiration Community, whose grace and remembering open the way to love.

Russ Hudson of the Enneagram Institute, whose knowledge and heart inspire me to dig a little deeper and sit a little longer.

Vimala Rodgers of IIHS.com, who taught me to write long hand, turn my paper landscape, and to cross my t's high. Yes most of this book was written longhand first.

Karen Curry of Indigo Heart Publishing, whose energy, joyful guidance, and insights were just what I needed to get this book written.

My Muse, that unnamed source of words and ideas that flow through me with the deep desire to be of service to others.

And lastly the thousands of people whose paths have crossed mine, inspiring a question and sometimes an answer.

About the Author

Deborah has been teaching, coaching, and writing since 1990 in topics ranging from total quality management to conscious parenting. She currently lives in Maryland with her husband, children, and two German Shepherds. She spends most of her time being with her family, working with clients, and exploring illuminating topics such as the Enneagram, Human Design, EFT, Unschooling, Homeopathy, and of course Family Energetics. Her blog and other information can be found at her site.

www.DeborahDonndelinger.com

Made in the USA
Lexington, KY
22 February 2015